Advance Pi
Million Dollar Adjustments

"I loved this book! It was a great way to look at disruption and change, breaking down learning opportunities and how to remove barriers to success. A very good read."

—Ozzie Guillén Jr., Producer of *Being Guillén*,
Host of La Vida Baseball

"An inspiring and timely message packed with powerful tools, *Million Dollar Adjustments* provides a blueprint to achieve goals as well as navigate inevitable change and uncertainty without stress or anxiety. This is a book this generation needs."

—Jordan Lee Dooley, *Wall Street Journal* Bestselling Author
of *Own Your Everyday*

"The Adjustment Awareness Audit is a genius tool for anyone in any industry. In just a couple of chapters, I discovered so much about my own adjustment style—more than I ever thought I would! This book is a must-read."

—Elizabeth Loutfi, Managing Editor, Chief Learning Officer

"Our lives are constantly being challenged, questioned, and thus prone to change. As an artist, I feel it's extremely important to keep current and make adjustments or we risk not connecting, becoming stagnant, or worse, simply irrelevant. This book will help anyone become a 'climber' and not merely a 'camper' and so I highly recommend it. If we don't evolve, we could dissolve."

—Michael Tait, Newsboys

MILLION
DOLLAR
ADJUSTMENTS

MILLION DOLLAR ADJUSTMENTS

THE POWER OF SMALL CHANGES

ON PERFORMANCE, PRODUCTIVITY,

AND PEACE

LINDA WAWRZYNIAK

A POST HILL PRESS BOOK

Million Dollar Adjustments:
The Power of Small Changes on Performance, Productivity, and Peace
© 2021 by Linda Wawrzyniak
All Rights Reserved

ISBN: 978-1-63758-016-5
ISBN (eBook): 978-1-63758-017-2

Cover art by Tiffani Shea
Interior design and composition by Greg Johnson, Textbook Perfect

Post Hill Press
New York • Nashville
posthillpress.com

Published in the United States of America
Printed in Canada
1 2 3 4 5 6 7 8 9 10

Contents

CHAPTER 1

Face to Face with Failure

*"I never blame myself when I'm not hitting.
I just blame the bat and if it keeps up, I change bats."*

—YOGI BERRA

Rafi looked at me with big brown eyes, waiting for me to say something that would ease his deepest worries and greatest fears. I wasn't his boss, and I had no power whatsoever to give him assurance about anything, but here he was, seeking it: the magical words that would assure him he was not about to lose his job. But I had none to offer.

Even though I tried my best to come up with an impactful "pep talk," it was off. Way off. Even as the words were coming out of my mouth, I knew that I had failed him. He was only twenty years old, miles away from his home country, unable to speak fluent English, and about to lose the only sense of financial security he had. While I didn't have the power to determine his job status, I could have helped him work through it and maybe even turn it around. But back then, I just didn't know how.

I wasn't even planning on talking with Raphael that day after English class. I didn't know that he would come up and ask to talk to me after all the guys had left. Putting away the class materials as usual, I realized he needed help only when he approached with a sad look in his eyes.

Standing at six foot three, Raphael, or Rafi for short, was a right-handed pitcher for a Class A professional baseball team. He was from the Dominican Republic, and I was helping him and his Spanish-speaking teammates learn English. His heart was heavy when he approached me and, in his broken English, said, "I not pitching good, teacher."

I knew instantly where he was going with this. When a player is in a consistently poor pattern of performance, he doesn't have much time to turn it around. Performance is constantly being monitored in professional sports, and players like Rafi must "make adjustments" within a short amount of time and improve or risk being cut from the team.

Raphael feared this was his imminent fate because he knew his performance wasn't as good as it should be. Being released is a real concern for players, especially in the minor leagues. This means they will not have an income or have a chance at their dream of making it to the big leagues. In addition, they feel as if they have failed themselves and their families, who believe this is their only opportunity for a better life.

I have seen many strong, grown men break down and cry after they have been released from playing baseball. It is very, very deep for them because, for many, it's all they know. It's what they love. It's their passion and sometimes their identity. For players from developing countries like the Dominican Republic, professional baseball is their ticket to feed their families, elevate their community, and lift them out of poverty. Most don't have an education or something else to fall back on. So when I see someone cry out of what the loss from failure brings, my heart breaks.

In those moments, we all seek out someone to turn our descent around, to help us regain our confidence or correct our course. I was Raphael's person. At that moment, my thoughts raced. What do I say to help him? After asking him if he had talked with his coaches and hearing him repeat their standard replies, I tried telling him a motivational story and made some analogy about how iron is refined by fire to remove impurities in the metal. Even though he was in the heat right now, I assured him he would come out stronger on the other side.

Rafi was released a week later.

Striking Out

My heart sank when I heard that news. Rafi's pitching never got back to the level it needed to, and the team decided that his time trying to get it there was up. Coaches and trainers know that unless there's an injury and the body isn't working properly, underperforming generally results from a problem of the mind. Rafi didn't have a way to unblock his failure and make the appropriate adjustments on the field. He didn't have someone available like this on the team who also understood the multicultural challenges of international players.

Thinking back to that day in class, I still feel partially responsible because I didn't have the right tools to draw from and help him in this situation. I was using old, partially developed tactics that I had stored in the back of my mind from somewhere in my past. These tools weren't the right ones for this situation. Maybe they were never the right ones, but they were the only ones I had at the time.

When I was growing up in my Latin American household, we had our share of failure but rarely talked about it much because it was too uncomfortable and hard. When failure in myself or my siblings did erupt into tears of anger or frustration, we comforted each other the best we could, which helped us keep going but didn't address the cause of our distress. It was a warm, validating approach, but something was clearly missing.

Years later, I noticed that, as a wife and parent, I tended to fall back on the old methods I learned as a child. When my kids failed, there were pep talks, comforting embraces, and suggestions on what to do next time. But I had no real understanding of *why* they failed and assumed it was due to a lack of knowledge, maturity, or experience in that situation.

At that time, I'm sure that even if I did know why they failed, I would have been limited on what to do about it. So I did what a lot of parents do—we hope our kids can figure it out and do better next time. Even if we feel the nagging worry deep down, we don't know what else to do. We feel unequipped to offer practical solutions addressing larger issues.

We may ask other people in our situations or with more experience. I know I did. Most of those people told me, "Well, that's all you can do. They'll get over it." That seemed to be the conventional wisdom at the time. But it felt so cold and unsatisfying. This was confusing for me because one approach from my childhood was warm and comforting, the other was cold and aloof, but neither equipped me or my kids to improve. That was what I really needed—to be equipped to move forward and to equip others to move forward in a very real, tangible way.

When my kids were in early grade school, I started teaching in baseball, and that's how I eventually learned new tools. If I had known then what I know now, I think I could have helped Rafi.

But instead, he returned home to the Dominican Republic with few transferable skills and limited job opportunities.

Days after his release, I kept thinking, "What if I had been better prepared?" I had no idea at that time that a player would want me to give advice about his on-field performance. I wasn't even qualified, or so I thought. In fact, I was told by the team that I wasn't even supposed to talk about on-the-field English usage, let alone performance. Off-the-field English was supposed to be my focus, teaching things like how to order food at a restaurant, how to speak to the people in a hotel, and how to converse socially with teammates and coaches. I followed those guidelines, assuming everything would go exactly as I was told. Players would learn how to adapt to life in the United States, and everything would be peachy.

But that was not the case, not for Rafi and many others.

We were striking out.

The Pressure to Pivot

No one wants to strike out. After the first swing and miss, we all try to connect the next time. But without making any adjustments, when the next pitch comes at us in a split second, we're just as likely to swing and miss again. This is just as true in life as it is in baseball.

Have you ever been in a situation that you didn't count on, and suddenly, you have to perform? And not only that, but you also have to succeed? You have little to no preparation, no prior knowledge, no idea that you will be called upon, then—BAM!— it's right there, and you have to step up and hit a home run. Or at least get on base!

Life is so uncertain, isn't it? We don't always get a warning that something important or pivotal is about to happen, but we have to be ready to respond to it. This happens at work, in our homes, with our friends, and anywhere we go. It happens if we are trying to lose weight, get in shape, learn a new language, build better relationships, help our children cope, succeed at work, or anything else we attempt to do that isn't perfectly orchestrated for us. The pressure to pivot is with us daily.

As humans, most of us love it when someone else has figured out the details of uncertainty so that all we have to do is follow their steps. But what if we run into a situation where we don't agree with their steps or realize there are no steps in place? Just like with the coronavirus pandemic of 2020, we had numerous "authorities" instructing us on what to do, when to do it, and how to do it. Sometimes, though, their instructions contradicted one another or caused confusion instead of clarity. We were left to discern for ourselves who to trust, what to do, and how best to proceed safely before clear, preventive guidelines emerged.

When we are put in these situations, we fall back on what I call our "hind brain," that primal part of our raw self, and instinctively assess our options, choose one, and implement it without realizing all the implications or consequences. If we only have one or two choices, we're in a pickle because our possible successful outcomes are limited. Like choosing between a warm, comforting pep talk or a detached, "you'll get over it" approach.

What we need is a way to navigate those sudden "big moments" so that if we don't perform at our best, we don't have to fail, face the consequences, and label ourselves a big fat failure. Both Raphael and I felt a form of failure that day after class, but for different reasons. He was failing himself, and I was failing him. Failure makes us feel ashamed and broken, useless.

Some people feel anger, disgust, shortness of breath, and overwhelming emotional pain, which can lead to identity shifting. It's deep, and it's personal, and we no longer see ourselves—or anyone else—clearly. Seeing ourselves as a failure can stop us in our tracks and cause us to lose hope and confidence in ourselves. If we don't find a way to get through it, we can get stuck there. Once we're stuck, we begin to assume we will fail because that's what failures do.

Most people don't know how to help us if we are in a place of failure. They do what I did for Rafi. They may give us some form of inspiration with the best of intentions but don't know what else to offer to help us. Maybe they recommend a resource or two, which is also a wonderful intention, but we need something more. We need to know how to navigate failure with new tools. We need to know how to leverage instinctive opportunities for maximum results.

So we search and search. Some people will find an adequate tool, but most will not. If the failure or uncertainty is bad enough, they may self-medicate through unhealthy means. Or they may withdraw from trying at all, which stops them from learning, growing, and ever reaching their full potential. They stall out and resign themselves to regret.

Or they adjust and transform their mistakes into successful failures.

Successful Failures

I have learned that in times of uncertainty, when failure looms, or right after some kind of failure or disappointment, we have to make adjustments in order to go forward. Adjustments help us appreciate the timeless truth that we often overlook in the moment: *success isn't stability, and failure isn't forever.* Read that again—*slowly*. Out loud even.

Success isn't stability. No matter how wonderful the performance or great the achievement, it isn't stable or guaranteed to continue. Once we reach a goal, it can change. We change. Circumstances change.

Failure isn't forever. Even when we don't hit the mark, this is also temporary. Once we accept that our attempt was just that—an attempt that did not achieve the desired result, then we can own it, learn from it, and, accordingly, make some change in our next attempt.

This is the essence of adjustment. The instability of success and temporality of failure mean that we will always be adjusting our successes and failures throughout our entire lives.

Because of this, adjustment is one of the most treasured and powerful words you should have in your vocabulary. Why? Because instead of putting yourself or others through the expectation of immediate change and success, adjustment is the key to creating successful steps that can help get you closer to where you want to go. Adjustments can even help you have a "successful" failure! Did you know that, yes, you can fail successfully? Imagine if you knew *how* to do that. Wouldn't you take a few more risks and feel a little more secure about yourself and your future? Wouldn't you be better equipped to help others who are "not pitching good"?

I want to show you how. Because I know without a doubt the power adjustments can have on a person's performance, attitude, success rate, and overall happiness in life.

I know that's a big promise, and I've been just as skeptical as you may be right now. In fact, the word "adjustment" was not one I used much before teaching professional athletes in baseball.

It seemed pretty vague to me—adjust what, where, when, and how? Adjustment was a *blah* word, a catchall kind of placeholder, which meant I had zero attachment to it or interest in using it.

One key conversation changed all that.

Patience and Adjustment

I remember it distinctly because it was my first spring training inside of a professional baseball camp. It was a scorching day in the Arizona sun, and all I could see were baseball diamonds and uniformed players foregrounded against the distant mountains. Sounds of bats cracking, balls sinking into gloves, and cleats spewing gravel filled my ears.

I had no idea what to expect as I walked around the baseball diamonds. There was hardly any talking, and everyone was laser focused. Coaches watched players with the same intensity with which players performed their positions. I felt a little intimidated by the seriousness and heavy testosterone hanging in the air. Knowing that this was minor-league camp, I didn't expect it to be so intense because the only frame of reference I had was the Single-A baseball practices I had seen in my hometown. They had been more laid-back and easygoing.

I soon learned that all players in spring training who had hoped to make it to the big leagues were "trying out" every day, even though they were already part of the organization. They were trying for a higher team that would get them closer to the big leagues, or for the big leagues themselves. For reference, an organization is the name you may know, like the New York Yankees or Los Angeles Angels. But the team is comprised of all players, both those in the minor leagues as well as the majors. The major-league teams are, of course, the top tier among all players in an organization, and their games are televised on most major sports networks. Starting on a Major League Baseball team is the pinnacle of every player's career.

That afternoon in spring training, as beads of sweat started to form on my forehead from the heat, a member of the team came up to me as I was watching practice to casually say hello. He looked a little older than the players on the field and introduced himself as Dave Hansen.

After we talked briefly about each other's roles, he told me he was a hitting coordinator and a former big-league player. I was immediately surprised and tried not to show it. A former big-league player here? Why would a former big-league player be in a minor-league spring training camp, even as a coach? Looking back, such thinking was a "rookie" mistake. It makes total sense that a former major-league player would know how to coach the next generation of players and enjoy sharing their career wisdom. But at that time, I had never met a big-league player before, let alone had a casual conversation with one. Fortunately, I resisted the urge to ask for a picture or an autograph!

Instead, with this rare opportunity in front of me, I asked Dave what his years in baseball had taught him. He talked a little about the game, but then he said something that I will never forget: "Through baseball, I've learned that life is about patience and adjustment."

It was so simple yet so profound. I guess I was expecting something about conducting television interviews, traveling on the road, or enduring the grind of the season. These are the things you think of when you think of a professional athlete: the glamour, the work, the celebrity status on a world stage. I never expected him to boil it down to *patience* and *adjustment*.

He shared how his career was transformed by these two simple principles, first as a major-league player for fifteen years and then transitioning to a coach and consultant. As a player, he was traded to a handful of teams, and as a coach, he contributed to several teams as well. All of these moves meant adjustment. I didn't know it at the time, but I met him during his first coaching job. Neither he nor I knew that he would move to coach other teams, but regardless of where he landed, Dave would be applying patience and adjustment.

Minor Adjustment, Major Impact

That one simple statement took me on a journey that I could never have anticipated. I became intrigued with this idea of adjustment and what it meant for baseball players and life in general, especially when I thought about it against the backdrop of my own life and those of others that I loved. I noticed that throughout my first few years of working with players, coaches, staff members, and trainers, the word "adjustment" kept resurfacing. It was insiders' lingo with enormous ramifications that everyone seemed to know except me.

No one said "failure" because failure was a given. In front of family, friends, and tens of thousands of fans, and on national television, no less, every player in the game knew failure was going to happen. While that could have been the primary focus, everyone in baseball talked about adjustment because they clearly believed it was more important—especially after every failure. And failure happened every day.

So what exactly was this adjustment thing?

Was adjustment just about getting a little better every day with more practice? Or was there more to it than that? I knew I had to dive deeper into this idea because it was clearly the secret ingredient to success, both on and off the field, for players and fans alike.

Over the course of many years, I started to unravel the secret of adjustment and now understand why it is the key to the highest levels of performance. Adjustment is definitely not a *blah* word or ambiguous idea. The impact of adjustment is much, much more.

After creating a few tools that helped me see how adjustments are made, I realized how powerful they could be. Now, within these pages, I will share these never-before-revealed tools to help you be prepared and equipped for whatever the future brings. If you or someone you love happens to fail in the future, I want you to be able to fail successfully and keep moving forward. That's the essence of a million dollar adjustment—making small changes with enormous impact!

When the heat of the moment is on you, and you're not sure what to do, then you need to learn about how to make great adjustments. If you have just failed yourself or someone else, then this is also the time for you to learn about adjustments. Just like I was, you may be giving yourself or someone else the wrong pep talk.

We are in uncertain times, and this can leave us all a little fearful. Fear can cause us to feel anxious, which can kill our confidence. But if you know how to adjust to new circumstances or situations, you can remain confident, move forward, and live the life you were made to live. You may not hit a home run every time, but if you're willing to make million dollar adjustments, I guarantee you will discover priceless benefits!

Are you ready to make your first adjustment? Then turn the page!

CHAPTER 2

What is Adjustment?

"It's unbelievable how much you don't know about
the game you've been playing all your life."

—MICKEY MANTLE

Spring training is a busy time of year in the world of professional baseball for coaches as well as players. Not only are they working to help get players ready for the season, but they also have many meetings to discuss how players are progressing.

The first time I was asked to attend one of these meetings, I quickly learned that each and every player would be discussed and evaluated on various levels. With a roster of over one hundred players to evaluate, you can imagine how long this confidential meeting went. I remember feeling hungry several times in those eight hours! Any coach, trainer, mental skills or education staff who had worked with players were invited to share pertinent information about strengths and weaknesses in order for the organization to help determine the very best plan for everyone's development.

As player names were called out, I heard various comments regarding skills, stats, and other observations. I also heard comments like, "He adjusts well," or, "He has a hard time making adjustments." I heard this over and over again. Here was that word from my first spring training! These comments were almost always followed up with examples of that player's performance in a game or practice. By listening to the examples of what was a "good" or "bad" adjustment, I started to realize that adjustment determined performance success or failure.

I thought, "Holy cow, what is it about adjustment itself that is so critical to a successful outcome?"

This question made me think about the connection between failed effort and success. While we all want to be great at our first attempts at everything we do, this doesn't normally happen for most people. Have you ever wondered what you could do to improve your chances for success in something? Things like work hard, follow all the rules, learn constantly, and be a good problem-solver and communicator probably top your list.

While these things do improve your chances for success, each requires a process to achieve it. In any process, no matter what it is, uncertainty will occur, things will change, or something might fail, and there will almost always be a need to make adjustments. Adjustment is the common denominator, the one thing that underlies almost anything you take on. This is what makes it so important and why it made sense that adjustment was part of the evaluation of high-performance people. It is also why it is so important to all of us.

Since that first meeting in spring training so many years ago, player evaluations have evolved with the advancement of technology and stats. Evaluation is more sophisticated, which only adds to, rather than takes away from, the need to make great adjustments. The reason is that now there needs to be a bridge between the metrics and the movements. Isn't that the same for all of us? Metrics are everywhere, and we are in a constant state of adjusting our processes or methods to keep up. While this sounds stressful, it doesn't have to be. Great adjusters are calm. You may be wondering, what makes a great adjustment?

Let's take a closer look at what elements influence every adjustment we make.

The Five Elements of Adjustment

After that first meeting, I was curious about this mysterious word, and I asked several coaches if they could tell me what they meant by "adjustment," especially in the context they were using it in. I had always thought about adjustment as a simple movement to make something easier or more effective, like what I did to the rearview mirror when I got in a different car. My simple idea was that adjustment was a small change you made when you needed to get better. I'm sure you may even think of adjustment this way too. I never thought of it as the key to success for a world-class athlete. Nor did I understand the many things that played into it. What was I missing?

Most of the coaches who I asked to define adjustment couldn't do it. I heard examples and words like "feel" and "see," but I didn't get much more. I didn't hear anything about change. I thought that was odd. When I asked them if they could see it after a failed performance in a game or practice, they would say, "Yes, but sometimes you can see it in a player's daily work too." Much later, I learned that no one liked to use the word "change" because that insinuated that the player needed to do something entirely different. Players didn't get to the pro level without talent, so no one wanted to change much. Adjusting what they already had was good coaching.

Intrigued by the idea of building on what was already there, I took the idea of adjustment back with me into the classroom after that meeting. I started experimenting with how to make players better "adjusters" through learning because this was the area that I controlled and seemed to be a skill that could help them. Players didn't have a lot of time to learn in the world of pro sports, so if I could speed it up, that would be beneficial to their career. To do that, I had to pull apart the concept into smaller pieces and study it so that it could be helpful.

After over ten years of research, testing, and trial and error, I found that adjustment is a type of modification in how we do things built on five key elements. These five elements work together in different ways, informing and inspiring individual behavior when it comes to new situations and repeated attempts at old ones.

Knowing these five will help you understand yourself and how to unlock an area that may have kept you stuck in the past. They are also the foundation of the Adjustment Awareness Audit, which you will see in chapter 4. The key five elements are Strategic Actions, Beliefs, Internal Timing, Information Synthesis, and Knowledge.

1. Strategic Actions

Before baseball, I had spent a lot of time in the corporate world and had had a few annual performance reviews with my superiors. Maybe you have had similar reviews in jobs you've held. In those corporate evaluations, I never remember hearing that I would advance in my job if I could make good adjustments. The focus was on doing tasks to mastery. Daily job responsibilities were discussed and graded according to how I was performing them. If I received a lower grade in an area, my supervisor and I discussed how I could improve. Each improvement was followed by an action step. For example, a poor grade in using a certain technology platform would be followed by the action step of attending training on the platform and spending more time learning it. Perhaps you've had similar action steps after your performance review.

Action steps that improve our lives are all over the internet, social media, books, and so on. You can find action steps on all topics. For example, the "3 Steps to Weight Loss," or the "5 Secrets of Better Relationships," and the "7 Ways to Build Wealth." These action steps simply provide you with a road map to help you see which adjustments you need to make to experience some success, but you have to *do them* to see the change you want.

If you're like me, you may do one or two of the steps on the list, and then life takes over, and you don't get to them all. Or maybe you do all of them, but then something happens, and you don't maintain them—especially if there is no strategy underpinning why you're taking the steps to begin with. This is the reason you hear motivational gurus tell you to define your "why." They are assuming that motivation to finish a series of steps, or get through a process, will come from a strong enough reason. While that may be true in the short term, that is still an outcome-focused mindset. Unless the "why" is mission-based, action steps alone for a short-term goal will not last over time. A mission provides a direction that a strategy is built from. We need both a mission and a strategy to accomplish the action steps and focus our effort. War is a great example of this.

Let's look a little closer at strategy and how strategic actions help us make good adjustments. A strategy is the process of chunking action steps into blocks and prioritizing their sequence. For example, a simple financial strategy would be getting out of debt from a loan and using that money to invest in something else. If my friend John says to me, "I'm going to pay off my car in one year to get out of debt," that requires him to make payments—one each month. It also requires 365 days of working to earn the income to make those payments. Unless John wins the lottery and pays off the car with just one check, he needs to do all of the above-mentioned action steps in a specific sequence to achieve the original strategy. If he misses a month of work, he won't be able to make a payment that month, and the original strategy will be off.

Great adjusters understand the importance of strategic action steps. However, strategic action steps by themselves are not what make us great adjusters. Creating and following strategic steps allow us to plan and do, and while those are good things, we need something more. If John misses a month of work, his timeline will change. What does John do to get back on track? The plan has to be adjusted. There are five elements in total, which means that in addition to strategic actions, there are four other things needed to be a great adjuster: beliefs, internal timing, information synthesis, and knowledge. Let's dig more into these elements.

2. Beliefs

If you've ever tried to teach someone something, you know that failure happens as a key part of learning. Maybe you were the learner, and you know this firsthand. Some form of failed effort is important because it helps refine our focus. When failure happens, the learner has to *want* to go back and figure out a way to "get it." S/he has to be motivated. Motivation is important because s/he also has to "see" something that was missed before, which takes some effort. Perhaps this is what the coaches were talking about? They knew that seeing the old methods against the new requires a certain type of vision as well as the effort to implement it.

If you can't "see" what's missing in a situation, frustration sets in and stalls motivation, and beliefs start to form. Self-talk becomes negative. "I can't pay off my car now," "I can't hit this baseball," "I can't lose this weight," "I can't do the right thing," and so on. It doesn't matter how many action steps are given or in which order. Belief will play a part in your drive to do something and, therefore, your effort and behavior.

Belief in our abilities comes from our internal translation cues. When effort doesn't translate into the desired outcome, we make judgments about our abilities. If a failed outcome continues, those judgments harden into Beliefs. This is dangerous if failure repeats itself because we can start to see ourselves as a chronic failure. The belief can become a label. For example, "I'm a failure at financial strategies." We can redeem this by looking at the truth of the situation.

The truth is, when we are just serving ourselves, our beliefs may be too self-centered. If we believe we can do anything we want, we can begin to see ourselves as more important than we should. We have to believe that we can make the adjustment, not just for glory or greed but to help ourselves or others grow in an important way. In my case, I had never played a game of professional baseball in my life. The extent of my experience was backyard baseball with my brothers and neighbors as a kid. When I decided that I needed to know more about baseball to help the players, I had to believe I could learn and acquire the skills I needed to do so. I had to grow my Belief element.

Perhaps this is why the world of sports uses the word "adjustments." It allows us to understand that the road to success is not a straight line. It's not one effort, one outcome. It's multiple efforts, various outcomes, altered efforts, other outcomes, and so on until we reach our goal. Our beliefs are not as flexible as we think they are and harden pretty quickly based on patterns we see in our environment or from childhood. Patterns often come from repetition. No doubt this was created in us to protect us from harm. But sometimes we can be unaware of how hard they have actually become.

Beliefs represent what is happening around us and are a choice we make. These choices become our reality. Studies have shown that beliefs do, in fact, alter our biochemistry.[1] This has been proven by many studies that use placebos. We know that when we change our thinking, we change our beliefs. And when we change our beliefs, we can change our behaviors.

The beauty of a good adjustment is that it acts like a grace period. It's the in-between area before beliefs are hardened. If we can pause time after failure, uncertainty, change, or emotionally charged situations and step into a place where we can get a "do-over" with a new technique, then we give our brains a chance to hold off on hardening that pattern for a bit. We are, in essence, hovering between an effort and its outcome. With this type of hover comes no labels because the outcome has not yet happened. It's not the same as merely passively waiting. It's an intentional gray area of time. True adjusters, those who experience great success, keep negative beliefs from hardening too quickly by allowing themselves to step into this active grey area.

---

[1] T. S. Sathyanarayana Rao et al., "The Biochemistry of Belief," *Indian Journal of Psychiatry* 51, no. 4 (October-December 2009): 239–41. https://doi:10.4103/0019-5545.58285.

In the grey area, you realize that the outcome happened, but you can try again. You're not past the window of success or growth.

This is the place where we believe in the impossible. This is the green grass of hope.

3. Internal Timing

In looking at the adjustment test data, it was extraordinary how much time varied by each individual. In order to understand the process of adjustment, we have to have a new understanding of time. We have to know how our mind keeps time.

Most people think of time as linear and chronological. This is true in that time goes forward. There are twenty-four hours in a day, and each hour has sixty minutes. Our clocks provide us the mark of time by minutes and seconds. Overall time is governed by the movement of the planet, and the natural world responds to that. Our bodies move to rhythms. For example, most of us sleep when it's dark and work when there is light (unless you work the night shift!).

In order to suspend our beliefs and desired outcomes, as was just mentioned under the section about beliefs, we have to understand our biology in terms of time.

To make this more understandable, let me compare it with teaching language. When teaching someone a foreign language, just like when teaching music, there is a "beat" or "rhythm" that must be learned. Words have syllables and "hold time." For example, the word "star" is one syllable in English. But when Spanish speakers try to say it, some add an extra syllable at the beginning. They say "eh-star" (like "español"). The reason is that the letter "s" in Spanish isn't as hard as it is in English. Spanish speakers have to work hard on this syllable difference when learning the rhythm and timing of the language. It was an important part of my work to teach players how to use these rhythms to learn English quickly. In trying to do this, I began researching language timing and stumbled upon "brain time."

Before clocks were invented, our bodies kept time, but in a different way. This is an amazing part of our biology. In a very simplistic explanation, we use the pulses in our brains to give us our perception of time. Think of how some life events seem to go in slow motion (like witnessing a car crash or daydreaming) or speed up (dancing with someone you are attracted to). These types of events send chemicals to our brains through our central nervous system and speed up our pulses or slow them down.[2] I call this Internal Timing.

Internal timing plays a big part in how we make adjustments because it is the element that allows us to pause our beliefs long enough to try again (the grey area). Through my testing, I have seen firsthand how internal timing plays a part in how people handle new situations and attempt to adjust to failed attempts at things.

While beliefs are formed based on past experiences, cultural norms, and ideals, internal timing is regulated by our DNA, emotions, health, and disciplined training. Internal timing is so individualized and subtle that most of us are not even aware of it.

Extensive research has found that as humans, we all have different "beats" pulsing in our brains, which means time has different nuances for all of us. When working through a strategy, like paying off our car in a year, for example, we execute most comfortably at our own tempo.

---

[2] Rhailana Fontes et al., "Time Perception Mechanisms at Central Nervous System," *Neurology International* 8, no. 1 (April 2016). https://doi:10.4081/ni.2016.5939.

Internal timing is an ongoing activity, and it will tend to drift if left alone. This is why athletes like to listen to music before a game to set and speed up their rhythm.

My friend John may be highly motivated to pay off his car in one year, but it's important to ask, how is his internal timing? Using a metronome, we find that he is most comfortable going through life at a speed of one hundred beats per minute. This is his natural tempo.

Unfortunately, his job requires higher productivity, and he has to work at a speed of 120 beats per minute in order to get it done in time. This causes him to miss some deadlines, and his boss isn't happy. His hours get cut, and someone else gets part of his work. Now John will not make his financial goal of paying off his car in one year unless he can earn more income. If John does nothing to adjust his internal timing, he will keep experiencing similar outcomes, which will affect his beliefs, his strategies, and, eventually, his life.

This works the same for you and any goal or outcome you are working toward. Internal timing is what allows us to be productive and yet suspend harsh judgments about ourselves, others, or situations. We can speed up or wait, depending on the situation. We can't aim for the "quick fix." Instead, we must work toward the "right fix." This type of time is run by our thoughts and biology, not by the hands of the clock. Patience is about internal timing.

When chronological time collides with internal timing, this can create anxiety. For example, if you are waiting for something to happen, and it's not happening at the pace you would like, this misalignment is uncomfortable. Doubt can creep in and cause us to do things in haste or slow down to a crawl. Great adjustments happen when we take note of chronological time but understand internal timing (and eternal timing) is at play!

4. Information Synthesis

The word synthesize simply means to scan, pull apart, and arrange or combine. When we are in a new situation, face obstacles, or hear new information, our brain will scan what is new, pull out the patterns we already know, and start to arrange this information in ways that are valuable and useful to us. For example, if you have to take a new route to get to a familiar place due to a detour, you might look for bigger landmarks like a water tower or a mountain range to help orient you and find that new route.

Sometimes someone else will help us do this, like a coach, mentor, parent, or boss. This can be especially helpful if we are in a stressful situation because our thinking may not be clear. Mental skills coaches will often teach breathing techniques to athletes to slow down their thinking so they can regain control emotionally. Once we are back in control, we are ready to see the information again and synthesize it for our benefit or the benefit of others. One great benefit of synthesizing information is that it helps with our focus. We need focus to recognize patterns hiding in information and rearrange them into something useful.

When coaches told me that they could tell if someone was a good adjuster or not, I realized that they looked at how quickly players could synthesize information while they played in order to change strategies if they needed to. I'm not sure if *they* realized that this is what they were looking at, but reading cues from the environment plays a big part in how we react to them.

Emotions come from past experiences as well, and certain events can bring them to the surface. If we have strong information synthesis skills, we have a good chance of staying in control because we are focusing on facts and how to use them to move forward rather than getting caught up in an emotional spiral.

One of the things I've learned from testing and teaching players is that we, as a culture, don't spend enough time teaching information synthesis—especially in stressful situations. Great adjusters have learned this skill. They look for and see patterns, clues, and information in their environment and use them to reach their goals.

5. Knowledge

Some of the best players in the game spend a lot of time watching videos of their performances. Why do they do this? They want to see what they did well and what they didn't in order to improve. All of this adds to their current knowledge.

Merriam-Webster defines knowledge as the range of one's information or understanding, gained through experience or association.[3] We need knowledge to get better at something. We increase knowledge through exposure time, which strengthens pathways in the brain. In essence, it's how we learn.

We also need knowledge so that we can pull learned information out of our memory when it will help us in a new situation. For example, hitters cannot always see the ball the entire way through the pitch. So, in their mind, they fill in the path the ball is taking with knowledge of what they last saw and memory of what this usually means at the plate. Filling in with the memories gained through knowledge learned is common as we attempt to do something.

Some people think instinct is some magical skill. But in reality, instinct is long-term memory put into action.

---

[3] *Merriam-Webster*, s.v. "knowledge (n.)," https://www.merriam-webster.com/dictionary/knowledge.

Think about the simple idea of touching a hot stove. If you touch it when it's hot and burn your finger, you learn that stoves can be hot. In the future, you instinctively know not to touch it, and you pull back your finger. All learning changes the brain and can change the heart as well. Some people learn action and consequence faster than others, meaning they need less repetition and exposure to it in order to learn it and put it in their memory for later retrieval.

Everyone Has Patterns

Today, speed tends to rule. We are bombarded by information, new tools and methods, the needs of others, and so on. And as humans, we work to keep up. This can knock our goals off track. So being able to adjust quickly matters. This is why we need to know our pattern and the five elements that influence it.

Once the five basic elements of adjustment were uncovered, I started experimenting with them in the classroom. I worked with a statistician, and we compared this information to on-field performance. It was no surprise to learn that they matched over 70 percent of the time. I once heard a financial guru say, "How you do anything is how you do everything," and after seeing adjustment patterns in people, I realized how true that statement was. Everyone has patterns of adjustment without realizing it.

When you know your patterns and can make good adjustments, you tend to be more creative, relaxed, productive, confident, and less anxious. The reason is simple. You don't worry about the quick fix anymore. You don't fear failure as much. You get more focused on what makes sense. You roll with uncertainty because you have confidence and hope in the future.

I've seen great athletes experience failure. When they saw how they made adjustments, they were immediately surprised. I showed them how to use this information in their favor, and they got back on track. In addition, they were calmer, happier, and felt more in control.

Failure isn't the only time we need to know what our adjustment pattern is. We need to know it to help us navigate change, uncertainty, and even detrimental temptations. Once you know your pattern, it is immediately clear how you tend to reach your goals. Whether your goal is paying off a car, losing weight, improving a marriage, staying strong in your faith, or making the big leagues, these outcomes require hundreds or even thousands of adjustments. Some of those adjustments will be big, and some will be small, but they will all make up the bridge between where we are now and where we want to go. The game of life has many unexpected twists and turns, so let's get ready for them!

CHAPTER 3

How Today's Disruptors and Drivers Impact Adjustment

"The greatest thing about baseball is that there's a crisis every day."

—GABE PAUL

In the recent past, we have seen many changes in the US and the world. The term "new normal" began circulating in early 2020 during the COVID-19 pandemic, and at that time, no one knew the full impact of what that meant. The term "new normal" is a bit of an oxymoron because "normal" means what is usual or the same. But the word "new" means something different. In 2020, the new normal just meant "things are about to change."

It was ironic that I happened to be in spring training camp the day I heard the news that MLB was shutting down all games. Big things always seemed to happen in spring training! It was a surreal moment. One day, we were all having meetings, talking on the field, eating in the team cafeteria, and so on, and the next day, everyone was packing up and going home. The media swarmed the building to get interviews with players or staff and see what they could learn, but everyone was tight-lipped. The next day, on Friday the thirteenth, I got on a plane to go home. The rest of the baseball season was disrupted by the health crisis, and everyone was wondering when it would start up again. Different ideas were tossed around, and I heard one older coach say that he didn't think it would be played at all—at least not without major adjustments. At the time, I thought, "No way!" but it turned out that he was right.

The truth is that people have been making big adjustments for many years prior to the pandemic. I'm sure you've experienced this in your life as well. Normal life was slowly being disrupted with innovations at work and home, but the pandemic created a disruption climax. I can't think of one person who told me they didn't feel some disruption to their normal life during 2020. I'm sure the same is true for you.

When you think about adjustment, how does that make you feel? Does it feel like a change? Is that exciting, or is it a little scary? Some changes can be exciting, while some aren't. Have you ever wondered why that is?

It comes down to effort and how it impacts our comfort, happiness, goals, or mission. If the effort we need to give moves us closer to what we want, we can say our efforts were worth it or that they "paid off." We may be more motivated to embrace adjustment, which could lead to change in that situation.

What if the payoff isn't worth the effort to us? What if we don't have a choice in the matter?

Forced change can disrupt our comfort and our lives. Sometimes it can even feel like it's controlling us. We may find ourselves in a place where we have to adjust merely to survive or meet our goals. This can be a difficult place to be in.

The fact is that disruptors are all around us. We can expect to be exposed to them in our lives fairly often. Disruptors and drivers are two of the biggest things that create the need to make adjustments and force us to evaluate the payoff of those adjustments. Let's take a closer look at both of these.

Disruptors

A disruptor is anything that interrupts our idea of "normal." Disruptors can occur in our work or personal lives. They are usually due to an innovation or life change. They can be positive (like getting married or buying a new car), or they can be negative (like job loss or death). A batter who can hit a pitcher's best fastball is a disruptor to the pitcher. The bigger the disruptor, the more adjustment is necessary.

Have you ever had a time when something disrupted your life? Did you feel a little nervous, anxious, or maybe even scared? You knew a change was coming, but were you *ready* for it?

Disruptors are part of life, and we all experience them. They are one of the key reasons we have to know our adjustment pattern. They act on one or all of the five elements of adjustment discussed in the last chapter and can create tension in the way we move through them. Let's look at some of the most common disruptors in today's environment. They are technology, energy and transportation, food production, dating/ relationships, and sports and entertainment. All of these areas impact our overall health and well-being in some way and, therefore, impact our behaviors.

Technology

Technology has exploded in the last fifteen years. With the invention of the internet and then the mobile internet, the devices and tools to deliver these networks have grown exponentially. We see tech products and services at the forefront of disruption. From smartwatches to mobile applications like Zoom and Waze, we see tech disrupting the simple way we used to do things.

Technology will continue to grow in many areas of our lives, including health, education, finance, and household products. Automation, artificial intelligence, nanotechnology, augmented reality, and the internet of things are examples of the next explosion in disruption.

Even money has changed from hard currency to more digital platforms like Venmo and cryptocurrencies. Paper coupons are now QR codes, and you no longer need a stamp or a checkbook to pay your bills (My husband wasn't happy about that one!). Money is seamlessly moved in and out of accounts with digital transactions. With the evolution of Bitcoin and blockchain technology, this trend in money disruption will continue to grow.

In your opinion, is the payoff from the use of technology worth the effort to learn it, buy it, and use it? If you think it is, this will help you begin to adjust to it. If not, your adjustment journey may be more difficult but worth it to you. This answer is different for everyone.

Energy & Transportation

According to *Inc.*, energy is going to change throughout this decade.[4] We will see less fossil fuel and more green energy like

---

[4] Soren Kaplan, "10 Disruptive Trends for 2020," *Inc.*, (February 5, 2020), https://www. inc.com/soren-kaplan/10-disruptive-trends-for-2020.html.

solar power. Think about what this means for transportation. More cars, trucks, and motorcycles will follow in the footsteps of Tesla, Inc. and run on battery power. We will most likely see more self-driving vehicles as well. This means there may be more stations to recharge batteries along the highway. Won't that be a crazy day when you can look over at the car on your left or right and not see a driver?

Pay-per-use bikes, mopeds, and scooters have already begun disrupting college campuses and large cities, changing how we get around and the energy we consume. With the recent disruptions of the taxi service through Uber, owning personal transportation may become a thing of the past. This is one way to free up some garage space!

Again, these disruptors will test our idea of payoff. We will ask ourselves if cleaner air and fewer vehicles on the road are worth the adjustments we will need to make in order to enjoy them. From recharging a car battery to downloading apps and waiting for a ride, these adjustments will take our effort in one area and place it in another. Again, the payoff for the adjustment effort is different for each person.

Food Production

According to many sources, the future of food will look different than it does today. Farmers are experimenting with vertical farming, which uses structures that grow crops indoors year-round using specialized lighting and water systems. New products and technologies in this area are disrupting traditional outdoor farming and will continue to do so.[5]

---

[5] Sarah Federman, "Vertical Farming for the Future," U.S. Department of Agriculture, (August 14, 2018), https://www.usda.gov/media/blog/2018/08/14/vertical-farming-future.

In addition, many food scientists are looking for ways to reduce the reliance on meat. Good Food Institute is an organization that works to develop alternatives to meat. Bruce Friedrich, of Good Food Institute, stated in a recent article in *The Guardian* that "by 2050, (almost) all meat products will be plant-based or cultivated." While plant-based meats are already here, cultivated meats will be more disruptive to today's meat-eaters. Cultivated meat is grown in a lab, developed from animal or fish cells in the nutrient bath of a "bioreactor."[6]

Going one step further, some predictions include the idea that microorganisms like yeast or microalgae will be grown in bioreactors and use 3-D technology to replicate the texture and taste of food. While this sounds like a scene from a science fiction movie, it is very possible that these disruptors will come. I think it will be interesting to see how our bodies adjust to the future of food!

Dating

Romantic relationships have been changing since the 1970s due to many factors (oral contraceptives, the feminist movement, condoms, speed dating, online dating, swiping left, sliding into DMs, and so forth). And while most of the other disruptors are about fast change, we will likely see a return to slow dating[7] as it was in the '50s. This means the disruptor will be disrupted, which can happen as well. Dating tools will probably always exist, but thoughts of tapping into the number of available people to

---

[6] Sirin Kale, "Food in 2050: Bacon Grown on Blades of Grass and Bioreactor Chicken Nuggets," The Guardian, (January 1, 2020), https://www.theguardian.com/food/2020/jan/01/food-in-2050-bacon-grown-on-blades-of-grass-and-bioreactor-chicken-nuggets.

[7] Tamara Rahoumi, "25 Ways Dating has Changed in the Last 5 Years," *Stacker*, (February 7, 2020), https://stacker.com/stories/3907/25-ways-dating-has-changed-last-50-years?page=3.

date may be replaced by focusing on the quality of a connection. I'm hopeful that this continues. The human heart will always be searching for love, and this will not change in the future.

It seems that with this emerging trend in slow dating, singles are finding the payoff of an intimate relationship with just one person worth the time and patience of finding the right one.

Sports & Entertainment

Sports and entertainment have been changing in recent years. Disruptors like team-owned television broadcasting channels and streaming have changed the ways viewers see and pay for sports content. In order to maximize the fan experience, sports teams will continue to interact with them through various means like real-time augmented reality stats on screens, and provide esports and fan districts as well as year-round social media engagement from athletes. Live sports events will change to ensure more safety protocols,[8] and athletes will have wearable technology.

Digital transformation is embraced by sports executives who want to have more data in order to make better investments and sustain higher profitability. Players are more aware of these statistical measures and are trying to adjust to meet these new benchmarks, sometimes creating a divide between a coach's experienced teaching and their need for more rapid improvement to meet these digital benchmarks.

Disruptors have also happened in other areas of entertainment, such as the movie industry. With the invention of VHS tapes and CDs, movies became more accessible and disrupted

---

[8] Pete Giorgio, "2021 Sports Industry Outlook," Deloitte, (2021), https://www2.deloitte.com/us/en/pages/technology-media-and-telecommunications/articles/sports-business-trends-disruption.html.

movie theaters. Then digital streaming became available, and new companies like Netflix created big disruptions in existing companies like Blockbuster Video, which built a mini-empire on recorded movies. Streaming companies have disrupted cable and satellite companies, and even more are on the horizon.[9]

Going forward, the movie industry will continue to move toward VOD (video on demand), and the type and length of movies may change as well. Too bad movie popcorn can't be on-demand too!

Is the convenience of watching games and movies on our devices whenever we want worth the effort of purchasing the technology needed instead of attending the live event altogether? Again, the answer to this question is different for every individual.

Drivers

Whereas a disruptor is something that *interrupts* our normal, a driver is something that *creates* a new normal through some sort of need or a change caused by a disruptor. A simple example of the difference between a disruptor and a driver is seen in the devices used to help people write. When the typewriter was invented, it disrupted the way people were writing with paper and pencil. Once it became affordable and people started buying more typewriters, the demand for ink, or "ribbons" as they were called, went up too. Businesses were created just to make those ribbons! Typewriters became a driver for the ink market.

---

[9] Chris Arckenberg et al., "Digital Media Trends: The Future of Movies," Deloitte, (December 10, 2020), https://www2.deloitte.com/us/en/insights/industry/technology/future-of-the-movie-industry.html.

When word processors took over for typewriters, that was another disruption, and people started learning how to use them. Because there was no way to print from a word processor, this created a new driver—the printer market!

More recently, the pandemic was a disruptor that changed our normal way of doing things. But then it became a driver because it created a surge in health-related products (masks, hand sanitizer, and gloves). War is another example of an event that both creates disruption and drives new products and services.

The economic shutdown that was mandated because of the pandemic caused people to leave big-city apartment living for single-home, suburban living. Investments in construction and home improvement increased, and more homes were produced. According to a CNBC article, sales of newly built, single-family homes were up 13 percent higher annually in May 2020.[10] We can say that the pandemic was a driver for home sales and residential products. This trend may continue if workers are allowed to continue to work remotely.

To Accept or Not to Accept

The choice of accepting the adjustments we may need to make in the face of disruptors and drivers is highly individualized, as pointed out. While change and uncertainty can cause anxiety and stress, resisting them too strongly may do the same as well, depending on what's at stake. Of course, there are situations when we can't adjust to everything that comes our way (see chapter 10). But constant resistance creates a different type

---

[10] Diana Olick, "Homebuilders See Strongest May Sales in Over a Decade, But They Have a Big Problem," CNBC, (June 23, 2020), https://www.cnbc.com/2020/06/23/homebuilders-see-strongest-may-sales-in-over-a-decade-but-they-have-a-big-problem.html.

of stress as well. This doesn't mean we should give in, by any means, if adjustments misalign strongly with our beliefs or abilities. Going the easy route isn't always the right one, and we have to weigh all the elements.

Each person has an adjustment threshold based on their pattern, or tendencies, and learning how to lean into it when your "normal" gets disrupted will allow you to make the right adjustments at the right time for yourself.

Since we have been making adjustments since we were babies, adjustment patterns have been etched in our brains. As creatures of habit, we do what has worked for us in the past. The problem is that disruptors are not created equal, and our learned pattern regarding how to handle them may not be effective in every situation. Whether it's a pitcher who has to find a new pitch to throw a talented batter or a musician who has to find a way to bring live music to an audience after the concert season has been canceled, there are always new challenges where we can win or lose.

Such was the case for a friend of mine who, as a music agent, faced the above situation with the 2020 concert season.

Backyard Music

In the spring of 2020, the music industry was disrupted due to COVID-19 because people were not allowed to gather in groups and, therefore, not able to go to concerts. Musicians who had tours scheduled throughout 2020 had to cancel them.

In late March 2020, I had a phone conversation with my friend Mike McCloskey, a music artist manager in Nashville, Tennessee. He is an accomplished Christian music industry veteran and has helped launch the careers of many well-established, platinum-selling, Grammy and Dove award-winning, *Billboard* chart-topping artists. In the years preceding the pandemic, through his role leading an artist management and recording label venture in Atlanta, Mike managed artist net tour revenue exceeding $25 million in the US and across five continents.

Mike shared that due to COVID-19, every tour date was canceled for all sixteen of his artists and the entire touring industry. He was scrambling to cancel or rebook hundreds of shows to the same time frame the following year, which seemed viable but not optimal, of course. The vaccine, it was hoped, would certainly help regain the confidence of attendees.

Many plans changed for so many people due to this virus. Perhaps you had many plans that were changed too. Was there a time when you had to figure out how to move forward after everything got put on hold? If so, you would have been in good company in 2020. A pandemic is a powerful example of the necessity of great adjustment skills.

Sometime in early August, I had another conversation with Mike. He shared with me that his musicians were going to be doing in total, more than one hundred exclusive and premium, high-dollar, private, backyard "home shows" for people who were interested. I told him I thought this was a great idea! I was so happy to hear of the adjustments Mike and his artists were able to do to continue bringing live music to people.

These backyard events allowed fans to personally connect with the artists, and something magical happened. They became more invested, and their connection grew stronger, which will probably make them lifelong fans. The musicians heard their fans' stories and were more inspired to serve them well. It was a win. Many of the artists, through hustle and adjustment, earned a net revenue comparable to the year before. The payoff was worth the effort, even though the definition of payoff looked different than a year earlier.

Our adjustment patterns help us know how we will handle big and small changes. They give us some information as to how long it's going to take us to figure out how to get through it and find alternative solutions. They also help us feel more confident in moving forward.

It might not surprise you to learn that Mike's adjustment pattern is a cross between what we call an All-Star and a Maverick. In short, this means that he is not going to get boxed in when change comes, and he will find a solution of some sort in order to move forward. This is exactly what he did with one of the biggest work disruptors he ever faced—total shutdown.

I didn't know Mike's pattern until months later when I asked if I could test him. When I explained to him what his results meant, he shared that knowing this gave him confidence, especially in light of some of the past struggles he had had.

You see, Mike had faced his share of failure over the years, even with such a strong adjustment pattern. Wait—isn't a good adjustment pattern a type of guarantee of more success? It definitely helps one succeed, but sometimes the problem is success itself or what we think success is. It depends on what each pattern's tendencies are. Let's go back to Mike's story to see what I mean.

Mike was living in Atlanta when he was fiercely tested. He was working as the executive vice president for a unique company that was a hybrid record label and artist management company. This hybrid company was a joint venture label with the global leading entertainment company, which was a little unusual. It would be like the New York Yankees hiring agents to represent their players. As I mentioned, it wasn't the norm.

In order to be successful, it required a lot of time on the road with musicians and constantly being with them. Mike put in the time and was very successful there. Things were going well. But his kids were growing, and he was missing many family events. In addition, his role was asking more from him, pushing him to his limits. Between the travel, the intensity of the role, and the constant pressure from his superiors, he began to get burned out. He couldn't enjoy his prior successes because the target was always moving higher and higher. Success wasn't celebrated. Instead, it was expected at the highest level at any cost. Mike was doing everything so well, but he was dying inside. He rarely saw his family and was beginning to lose himself in the futile attempt to be everything to everyone around him.

Everyone Wants to Be an All-Star

The All-Star pattern is one of the patterns that we have seen lead to great workplace success. All-Stars tend to see and do things at a higher level, and employers love them. While that could be the end of the story, it isn't. This person generally makes adjustments so well that others look to them for direction and give them more to do. If they aren't careful, they can burn out, as Mike did. All-Stars don't often have problems making adjustments, so if suddenly there's a new situation they can't navigate well, it can create extreme internal stress. Because Mike's pattern also has a strong Maverick tendency, the way his superiors wanted him to do things just didn't sit well with him. He felt there had to be a better way.

In 2016, Mike walked away from his prestigious job. In doing so, he lost many of the relationships he had made with people and felt the loneliness that unpopular decisions can create. He doubted himself, and his love of red wine became too tempting too often. Cabernet was a normal part of his work and home life in Atlanta. Between meals, award shows, meetings with clients and record labels, drinks with artists and bands, first-class flights, airport delays, hotel lobbies, and at home with his wife, it was a simple pleasure that was natural and easy. But with the uncertain circumstances and self-shame, things got a little out of hand for a short time. Fortunately, Mike was able to turn that around. He moved back to Nashville, where he had first started his career in the entertainment industry, and he now owns his own management company with another larger firm in the same town. He works with fewer artists but gets more enjoyment and life from these relationships. There is still success but also freedom and peace.

In order to get there, Mike had to make a series of adjustments with a pattern that was in a transformation stage. While in Atlanta, he was most likely still in an All-Star pattern. But it wasn't working for him. He had to realign his beliefs, his timing, his knowledge, and his strategic action steps all at the same time in order to win for himself and his family. This took some time, and of course, he didn't know anything about adjustment patterns. Perhaps if he had known his pattern and its tendencies at that time, he could have been better prepared to know his limits, change things more quickly, and, therefore, live more joyously sooner.

Benefits of Knowing Your Adjustment Pattern Tendencies

There can be some situations in life that will hit on several of the key adjustment elements at the same time, and when that happens, it can stop us. It can feel like we lost our way, and we may not know what to do to keep going. But this is where adjustment patterns can be strengthened and transformed to set us up to thrive in the future.

When we know our starting point and what plays into that, we can start to see where we can focus to stay strong and confident yet peaceful and calm in our response to things. Things can and will hit us, but we don't need to be knocked down very long—or even at all in some special cases.

Knowing more about your pattern and how to make great adjustments allows exciting things to happen. Having shared this powerful tool with people, I have seen several positive effects emerge. Here are some of the advantages of great adjustments:

1. Failure and uncertainty won't stop you. Disruptors will be less important.
2. Success will be more understood, attainable, and balanced.
3. Learning may come easier.
4. There will be a tendency to resist isolation from people because you will have more self-confidence. You might even become more social!
5. It will be easier to care about others because you won't be as worried about how you will take care of yourself.

You might experience one or all of these, depending on how well you know, understand, and maximize your adjustment pattern. These are not guaranteed; these are simply some of the outcomes I have seen when working with people who truly wanted to improve. Want to find out what your pattern could look like? It's waiting for you in the next chapter.

CHAPTER 4

Your Personal Adjustment Tendencies

*"Failure will never stand in the way of success
if you learn from it."*

—HANK AARON

The "Dumbos"

One of my favorite American coaches to work with was an older man named Joe, whose personality was a mix of the gruffness of an old gorilla and the kindness of a teddy bear. He had experienced success in his years as a coach, helping players get to championships many times. Joe was very interested in how players learned, and often, he would come to me and ask how a player was doing in the classroom. With his breadth of experience, he would make assumptions based on what he saw on the field and he would ask me to see if his impressions were confirmed in the classroom. I gave him a lot of credit for that.

But the first time it happened, it threw me off guard. I was in the Dominican Republic and was preparing to conduct an educational orientation for the players. He walked into the class, sat down, and said, "Linda, tell me about Felix. How's he doing?" In order to work with professional sports teams, I was required to sign very strict confidentiality agreements, so I was very guarded when it came to answering questions about player progress. Because of that, I answered his question with a question. "Well, Joe, what exactly are you asking me?" At this, he looked a little frustrated and quickly said, "I want to know if he's a dumbo or not." I was not expecting that answer!

I replied, "Well, he's making progress in class. What makes a 'dumbo' player anyway?" He looked me in the eyes and said, "You know, the guys who can't learn. The ones who probably didn't finish school."

It was in that conversation, and several others after that, that I realized the many times that players with minimal educational backgrounds were perceived as "dumbos," while the ones who had better educational backgrounds were perceived differently. In some ways, that made sense, and seemed like a logical conclusion.

Interestingly, I wasn't seeing the same thing in the classroom because I wasn't focusing solely on prior knowledge. I was also focusing on how players adjusted after failed attempts at applying learned information. I had seen that this was often a more accurate differentiator than past educational opportunities. I saw that every player brought learned patterns of post-failure and post-success into my class. Our adjustment pattern is part of our success process. When we have this information, it can be incorporated into our lives, and therefore, we will be less anxious about how we will confront failure, which I knew was important in learning.

The hard part for me was that it took half a season before I could see these patterns clearly enough to help optimize them. I looked for assessments that might be close, but most did not work well. They were either too language- and culture-heavy (which created a bias against non-English speakers because not all words translate the same in Spanish or other languages and therefore the true meaning may be lost), too digital, or weren't testing what was needed in order to truly help players. I realized that maybe we needed a new assessment. I leaned on my pre-baseball career to help. Assessment design was a key part of my career before baseball, so I was comfortable with this. I went to work on a prototype test.

Once I had a prototype test, I hired experts in testing protocols to help me write the plan, prerequisites, and acceptance criteria. Then the assessment was tested by gathering initial sample data and comparing it to performance outcomes. From there, more revisions were made, algorithms were written to verify the data, and protocols were updated. After many long hours and years of data set analysis, the resulting adjustment patterns were mathematically verified.

At the Plate

The test of adjustment was never originally meant to be used outside the classroom. I had a simple need to help international players learn faster so that language would not be a barrier to their success. However, one game in late July made me think about that a little more.

You see, when you teach athletes, you get to know them personally, and you want to see them succeed in their craft. I made it a practice to go to their games as much as I could to help support them and cheer them on. This was especially important to some because they were far from home and had no family members in the stands.

I had spent the morning testing one outfielder in particular, and his test showed me that he was having difficulty processing new information and executing it along with the old information. In other words, he didn't seem to be able to make adjustments well. As I watched the game unfold, he came to the plate. I crossed my fingers that he would get a great hit. He made contact the first time, but it was a foul ball. Then the pitcher made a change to the pitch and threw it hard. A swing and a miss. The umpire called, "STRIKE!" I saw that happen two more times, and he struck out. A thought occurred to me at that moment: "He isn't adjusting to new information on the field either!" It probably shouldn't have been a surprise, but it was. I started to wonder if there was some correlation between off-field adjustment performance outcomes and on-field ones.

I called Nick, the data scientist who wrote the algorithms, and asked him if he thought there might be a way to correlate the test results to on-field data. He said he could try it but didn't have access to data other than what was available on the internet. We both agreed that it made sense to start there. My expectations were low since we didn't know how "clean" the data on the internet was. Nick went to work setting up a few mathematical models to see what we might find.

The next day, I saw the coach of the team and asked him if I could ask a question about a player. He was very kind to say yes. I told him that I happened to notice that the player was having a hard time processing new information in class, and I asked if that same player was having a hard time on the field as well. He said that yes, this player wasn't making great adjustments!

I wondered if he had a way of measuring this, and he looked at me like I was from outer space. "Well, we can see it clearly every day," he said. Of course—observational information. No metrics existed besides performance stats around player actions, especially not player cognition.

I called Nick and shared this information with him. He said he had run a few models and told me to look at my email. I saw the initial modeling he made and the correlation values and couldn't believe it. It looked like the test to evaluate classroom performance outcomes was on par with on-field performance outcomes. That meant that if we could help players succeed with this information in the classroom, maybe it could help them succeed on the field.

Since classroom performance was on par with on-field performance, it only made sense to call the test the Performance Adjustment Response test, or PAR for short.

Over several years, the Signature PAR test continued to show us the *way* a player would tackle failure (and/or uncertainty) and *when* he would do it. This is so important when there is new material to learn, new situations to adapt to, uncertainty of outcomes, and possible failure.

You have already been part of a global pandemic, which meant many changes for you, your coworkers, your team, and, possibly, your family. Maybe these changes moved back the timeline on some things you were working towards, especially the things you have control of. Wouldn't it be nice to know something about your adjustment tendencies so that you could get back on track with your goals? Unfortunately, the Signature PAR test isn't available in a format that works within a book, but luckily general tendencies from test results have emerged. The results from this test are important to know, which is why this book was written.

But a book without an opportunity to self-evaluate or learn your own adjustment pattern doesn't make complete sense. A type of Signature PAR test in a different format was necessary. With this in mind, the personal Adjustment Awareness Audit (AAA) was born. It is not the same as the Signature PAR test, but it provides some important information about adjustment tendencies.

So, what is the Adjustment Awareness Audit? Let's start with the definition of an audit. An audit is a type of inspection, or review, of information to check for errors or omissions. If we audit our adjustment tendencies against highly successful adjustment tendencies, we can see where we have opportunities to grow and win. The AAA is a great tool to get this process started.

When I speak to people about adjustment tendencies, there are always a few elements that they weren't aware of, and suddenly, they find themselves in those elements. Many of us simply need to understand some of the basics.

While the AAA is a great tool to help you understand your performance adjustment tendencies, it should not be confused with the Signature PAR test. The reason is that during the Signature PAR test, the sympathetic nervous system is activated, showing us how the brain works during states of heightened stress. This is very difficult to do with paper-and-pencil-based tests. However, while the personal AAA isn't the same thing, it is a powerful first step in that it reveals your adjustment tendencies, thereby giving you information that can help you plan your next move so you can increase your odds of succeeding in your goals and God-given path.

Ready to learn more about your adjustment tendencies? Great! It's time. Grab a pencil or pen, get to a quiet place with no distractions, and dive in!

The Adjustment Awareness Audit

The Adjustment Awareness Audit is a series of fifteen questions. Read each question carefully and make sure you understand it before answering. Try to answer as honestly as you can. Remember, no one is going to "grade" your answers, and these are only for you to see. Once you feel comfortable with an answer, circle it or write it in the margin of the book. That will help you keep track when it's time to figure out your score at the end of the quiz. Take as much time as you need.

Answer the following questions:

1. Do you like new challenges?

   ☐ Yes   ☐ No   ☐ Sometimes

2. How often do you believe that you can succeed 95–100% of the time? Choose one.

   (very rarely to very often)

   ☐ 1   ☐ 2   ☐ 3   ☐ 4   ☐ 5

3. How much do you slow down when you need to work through a new problem? Choose one.

   (not at all to very much)

   ☐ 1   ☐ 2   ☐ 3   ☐ 4   ☐ 5

4. Which strategy do you prefer to use IMMEDIATELY after failing a new task?

   ☐ 1 I try to determine the true importance of the task

   ☐ 2 I simply try again

   ☐ 3 I try various other approaches

   ☐ 4 I try a completely different approach

   ☐ 5 I like to perfect one to two approaches that seemed to work best

5. When does time seem to speed up the most for you?

   ☐ 1 When I feel both internal and external pressure to perform

   ☐ 2 When I feel internal pressure to perform

   ☐ 3 When I feel external pressure to perform

   ☐ 4 When I'm thoroughly engaged in a productive activity

   ☐ 5 Time always seems to stay constant for me

6. How often do you accomplish the goals you set for yourself in the time you set them? Choose one.

   (not very often to very often)

   ☐ 1 ☐ 2 ☐ 3 ☐ 4 ☐ 5

7. How does your pace of talking compare to people around you?

   ☐ I talk faster. ☐ I talk slower. ☐ It's about the same.

8. When faced with a new challenge, what is your approach?

   ☐ I jump right in and figure it out as I go.

   ☐ I take a minute to study it first, and then I give it a try.

   ☐ I spend a lot of time learning about it.

9. How proactive/offensive are you when approaching a new task? Choose one.

   (not very proactive/offensive to very proactive/offensive)

   ☐ 1 ☐ 2 ☐ 3 ☐ 4 ☐ 5

10. How confident are you in your ability to accomplish your goals? Choose one.

   (low confidence to high confidence)

   ☐ 1 ☐ 2 ☐ 3 ☐ 4 ☐ 5

11. What percentage of the time are you reactive/defensive when approaching a new task? (*Reactive means that you act after something happens first. Defensive is used here to talk about a less aggressive strategy.*)

    ☐ 1 over 90% of the time I tend to be reactive/defensive

    ☐ 2 51–90% of the time I tend to be reactive/defensive

    ☐ 3 50% of the time I tend to be reactive/defensive

    ☐ 4 25–49% of the time I tend to be reactive/defensive

    ☐ 5 0–15% of the time I tend to be reactive/defensive

12. How often do you look for familiar information when attacking something new? Choose one.

    (very rarely to very often)

    ☐ 1 ☐ 2 ☐ 3 ☐ 4 ☐ 5

13. How often do you see the big picture importance of a task versus focusing on the task itself? Choose one.

    (very rarely to very often)

    ☐ 1 ☐ 2 ☐ 3 ☐ 4 ☐ 5

14. How much do you remember things you already did?

    ☐ 90% of the time

    ☐ 75% of the time

    ☐ 50% of the time

    ☐ 25% of the time

    ☐ less than 10% of the time.

15. How much do you enjoy learning things that can make your performance better? Choose one.

    (very little to very much)

    ☐ 1 ☐ 2 ☐ 3 ☐ 4 ☐ 5

Scoring Your Audit

In order to score your adjustment awareness audit, simply follow the directions below.

SECTION ONE

Please add your score for questions #2 and #10 and write the sum here. _____

Divide this total by 2 and put the final number here. _____

For example, if you answered 3 for #2 and 4 for #10, your total would be 7. When you divide by 2 your total score would be 3.5 for this section.

SECTION TWO

Please add your score for questions #3, #5 and #6 and write the sum here. _____

Divide this total by 3 and put the final number here. _____

This is your score for section two.

SECTION THREE

Please add your score for questions #4, #9 and #11 and write the sum here. _____

Divide this total by 3 and put the final number here. _____

This is your score for section three.

SECTION FOUR

Please add your score for questions #12 and #13 and write the sum here. _____

Divide this total by 2 and put the final number here. _____

This is your score for section four.

SECTION FIVE

Please record your score for question #15 here. _____

What Each Section Means

Section One: Beliefs

This first section focuses on our beliefs as they relate to making adjustments. Your audit score shows your tendencies when it comes to believing in your ability to make a successful adjustment. If you like new challenges, most likely it's because you feel you can succeed at them.

If you scored between 4 and 5 in this area, you most likely have a strong belief in your ability to make adjustments. Motivation is generally high, and possible failure isn't as daunting as the desire to succeed. Failure isn't at the forefront of your mind when you take on a new task. If you have a strong belief in your ability to adjust, but you haven't always had great adjustments, then it's possible your strategies, timing, or information synthesis may be the culprits holding you back from your goals.

Scoring a 3 or anything between a 3 and 4 means that your belief is situational, depending on what the potential for failure could be. Cautious optimism is a great way to describe your belief in adjustment outcomes. You have some doubts, mostly due to past circumstances or experiences. However, you are still willing to weigh the benefit of success and jump into the task. Recognizing doubts when they hit you and using refocusing techniques can be helpful to strengthen your belief.

Scoring a 1, 2, or 2.5 in this section means that you may doubt your ability to adjust to a new situation. Your doubts are due to more negative outcomes than positive ones in your past experiences. You may even have some fear regarding new things, and this could be holding you back from accomplishing your goals. Once you recognize the power that doubt or fear has on you, it is important to learn ways to overcome them.

How do you change the narrative in your mind when it comes to low belief? I have found that it has a lot to do with improving your timing, learning more offensive rather than defensive strategies, and knowing some key pieces of information that may be missing regarding the value of failing at times. In addition, low belief can stem from a heart that's been hurt. More on this in later chapters. But now, let's look at section two and see where your timing tendencies lie.

Section Two: Timing

This section focuses on our timing tendencies when it comes to making great adjustments. Your audit score in this area gives you an idea regarding how time plays a part in the execution of an adjustment. Time can speed up or slow down in our minds based on events and our emotional reactions to them. It is the brain's way of handling life and is dictated in great part by our biology. If you got bored with the audit after a few questions or were deeply immersed in it, your internal timing may be telling you something.

If you scored between a 4 and 5 in this section, you tend to balance time with accurate outcomes of the present task. You don't necessarily work too fast or too slow, you work to the needs of the task as well as the big picture. While time is important to you, you have learned how to control it so that you aren't ruled by it in a way that negatively affects your overall adjustment.

Positive, joyful events are the only ones that may impact your timing, and usually, these types of events don't require performance or if they do, these positive feelings can enhance it.

Scoring a 3 or anything between a 3 and 4 means that sometimes stress can creep in and throw off your timing. Some stress can be helpful to performance if it's in the right amount and at the right time, but when the amount of stress begins to increase too much or not enough, your timing goes along with it. You may notice that interruptions or distractions throw off your timing as well. Knowing your baseline time and learning how to train it can help keep it more consistent.

Scoring anything between a 2 or 3 means that while you may experience productivity, your timing may be causing stress and anxiety at greater levels. You may not feel in control of your time as much as you would prefer. There are things you probably want to do but don't ever feel like you have time for them because the time pressures are too strong. Knowing your baseline timing and altering some beliefs may help you make less stressful adjustments.

Scoring a 1, 2, or anything in between means that your internal timing may be impacting your ability to perform at a higher level. Pressure to succeed or a traumatic event may be slowing you down or stopping you altogether. You may notice you're not as productive as you would like to be and maybe you even feel a little low on energy. This is how internal timing can alter our ability to make adjustments.

Fortunately, internal timing can be "reset" through simple exercises. When strong internal timing is in sync with positive beliefs, performance increases, and we are more open to learning new strategies.

Section Three: Strategic Actions

This part of the AAA focuses on strategic tendencies as they relate to making adjustments. Whether you tend to jump right in to a new task or take some time to study it first, this says something about your best, or at least most comfortable, approach.

If you scored near a 5 in this section, you tend to take a calculated, offensive approach to adjustment. An offensive strategy is an action or plan that you initiate. A score near 5 means that you will find a good strategy and employ it often, making it become a "scoring" one. You don't wait to see what failure can bring. Instead, you stay on course and find ways to get a few strategies to work well for you.

If you scored near a 4 on this section, your approach is more offensive than defensive, but you are still working to determine the most successful actions or plan for you. While you are doing this, you are including some defensive strategies at times. A defensive strategy is an action or plan that is response driven. If you scored near a 4, you have found some success with what you are doing and can make it work as you adjust.

If you scored near a 3 on this section, many strategies are still being tested for success. You hover between offensive and defensive strategies, which may be what has worked best for you in the past. However, your strategy approach may not feel as strong as you would like it when new, unfamiliar tasks are presented. There is more trial and error, which could lead you to feel less in control at times.

If you scored near a 1 or 2 in this section, you have a stronger defensive approach to adjustment. Defensive strategies typically happen when there is greater uncertainty of outcomes and less desire to initiate a possible action, thereby reducing the perceived possibility of success. This is usually due to a lack of resources needed to initiate an action or plan.

Different situations call for different strategies, but we tend to employ the ones that work best based on past experience and the information we have at the time.

Section Four: Information Synthesis

As we learn from our past adjustments, we begin to establish patterns. We look for what we already know in a situation in order to have greater success. This section provides information on your tendency to synthesize, or scan, information as it relates to new adjustments.

If you scored between a 4 and 5 in this section, you tend to look for patterns and clues in new situations that will help you be most successful. You have good focus and can see how your adjustment will fit into your overall goals or the goals of others. The ability to scan a situation prior to making an adjustment allows for clearer steps on how to proceed.

Scoring a 3 or anything between a 3 and 4 means that you look for some familiar informational clues when making adjustments but that you may not need them. You tend to approach an adjustment with some flexibility as to what to expect and not make too many assumptions. Your scan may be quick and without detail.

Scoring a 1, 2, or 2.5 shows that your tendency toward information synthesis is to look at each adjustment as a new experience and not spend much thought scanning for clues. Information is always fresh, and adjustments are not focused on how one can be tied to another.

Some information can be useful when making adjustments. It's a matter of knowing how to pull out the pieces that are needed. Being able to do this quickly can help the strength of those adjustments. Prior knowledge is a beacon when it comes to wrapping up belief, timing, strategy, and information synthesis.

Section Five: Knowledge

Being able to gather, understand, recall, and apply information is another part of adjustment tendency. Information doesn't necessarily refer to "book" knowledge, but rather all knowledge, including experiential as well. We lean on what we know to help us navigate what we need to do.

If you scored a 4 or 5 in this section, you value knowledge and feel it equips you to make better adjustments. As long as knowledge isn't stopping you from action, it is a good ingredient in planning your strategic action steps. In fact, enjoying learning about how to make great adjustments is probably the reason you bought this book!

A score of 3 means that you prefer to learn some things but don't need too much knowledge in order to feel equipped to act. You may be a more experience-based learner, and if you interpreted this question as "book" knowledge, you may not have answered that you enjoy learning. While you may enjoy *some* book learning, most likely you enjoy *doing* just as much.

Scoring 1 or 2 points to tendencies against the idea of learning enjoyment as part of your adjustments. Again, you may have interpreted this question as "book" knowledge rather than learning through doing. However, the key word here is "enjoy." If you don't enjoy learning, you will make adjustments without searching for knowledge that can help you improve. Learning trauma does exist, and people who have experienced it can have difficulty enjoying learning, even if it can help them succeed.

Audit Scores and Adjustment Types

Now that you have an awareness of your adjustment tendencies, it's time to see how they fit into specific adjustment types. By zeroing in on your adjustment type, you will be able to understand how to optimize it and adjust to any situation.

First things first. Let's take a look at your tendencies and how they fit under various adjustment types. On to the next chapter!

CHAPTER 5

The Seven Types of Adjusters

*"Whoever wants to know the heart and mind of America
had better learn baseball."*

—JACQUES BARZUN

Self-discovery tools are readily available and accessible to just about anyone today. You can find information about how you do anything—from finding the best relationship match to work skills to health and wellness quotas. Classifying and labeling ourselves and others is a great way to gain insight into personal growth opportunities as well as how to develop others.

However, even if we know where we are and where we want to go, we still have to make adjustments to get there. Doesn't it make sense that this is where we should start?

If you just completed your Adjustment Awareness Audit in chapter 4, you probably want to know how your tendencies add up across all five sections. The tendencies of all sections combined give you an idea of what type of adjuster you are, meaning, how quickly and fully you will be able to gain new skills, navigate new situations, and move forward from what doesn't work.

In the data collected from all PAR testing, we found that seven common adjustment pattern types exist, with a few slight pattern outliers. We have learned that each pattern contains varying levels of the five key elements, as presented in chapter 2, and make up an adjustment pattern.

Matching Scores with Pattern Types

Let's take a look at the section scores from the AAA and match them up with pattern types. The chart on the following page allows you to quickly scan your various pattern type tendencies. Circle the pattern types that emerge in each section. If you have more than one pattern type for a section, circle all types. If you have one or more pattern types that seem stronger than others, then stay with these patterns.

For example, looking at the chart below, if you scored a 4.5 on section one, this is a tendency for the Maverick, Mock Maverick, and the Zipper patterns. Then if you scored 2.75 on section two, you would circle the Maverick and Mock Maverick Pattern Types.

If for section three, you scored a 3.67 on the AAA, you would circle the Mock Maverick and Steady Eddy types. Scoring a 3.5 on section four would put you at a Mock Maverick pattern and a 4 on section five would put you at the Maverick pattern.

Since most of your pattern tendencies fall under the Maverick and Mock Maverick tendencies, these would be your strongest tendencies.

AAA Pattern Type Tendency Identifier

Pattern Type	Section 1 Beliefs	Section 2 Timing	Section 3 Strategic Actions	Section 4 Information Synthesis	Section 5 Knowledge
All-Star	5	Nearer to 5	5	Nearer to 5	Nearer to 5
Maverick	Between 4 and 5	Nearer to 3	Between 4 and 5	Nearer to 4	Nearer to 4
Mock Maverick	Between 4 and 5	Nearer to 3	Between 3 and 4	Between 2.5 and 3.5	Nearer to 3
Zipper	Between 4 and 5	Between 4 and 5	Between 4 and 5	Between 4 and 5	Nearer to 5
Steady Eddy	3 or 4	Between 3 and 4	Between 3 and 4	Nearer to 3	Nearer to 3
Mascot	Nearer to 2	Nearer to 2	Between 1 and 2	Nearer to 2	Nearer to 3
Free Agent	Nearer to 1	1, or between a 1 and 2	Nearer to 1	Between 2 and 3	Between 1 and 2

Based on your section scores from the AAA, you can begin to see the various differences between the patterns. Whether you have the belief tendencies of a Zipper pattern type and timing tendencies of the Steady Eddy pattern type, they work together when involved in making an adjustment. Depending on the adjustment, you may need to strengthen your beliefs or better your timing, and therefore, these individual breakdowns and how they impact your next adjustment are very important to know. Each element as it relates to pattern types is explained in more detail:

Type One: The All-Star

Beliefs

An All-Star adjuster is a person who believes he/she can succeed and is motivated by doing things well. Through past experiences and positive self-talk, they have gained confidence in their abilities. They are not cocky but realistic and calm, believing that there is a way to make things work, especially if what they are doing is what they should be doing. For example, if an All-Star is trying to lose weight and get healthier, he/she believes it can be done and is not about thwarted by the effort it will take.

Failure isn't at the forefront of the All-Star's mind, but if it happens, encouragement and new techniques can generally get him/her back on track. If the All-Star who is trying to lose weight finds that nothing changes in week one, he/she will not give up.

Timing

Internal timing for an All-Star matches the thinking needs of a new situation or task. In other words, he/she may need a little more time at first to understand how to be successful but once this is known, he/she can generally do new things a little faster. In addition, All-Stars are known for their emotional consistency, which creates a consistent internal timing. Internal or external pressure does not seem to affect their timing in the negative. But joyful situations can briefly throw timing off track. However, the All-Star can be intense, so joy is also important to well-being.

When losing weight, if the All-Star has chosen the keto diet, he/she may take more time up front to plan out the meals and may wait on getting immediate results up front. But after multiple days and weeks of the diet, he/she will not need as much time to get weight loss results because planning and execution will go faster.

Strategic Actions

The All-Star is open to learning opportunities and has tried various success strategies as a result of this. All-Stars tend to be multistrategic and apply the actions that seem to work best in new situations. It is important to an All-Star to have options and strategies, or they can get stuck.

In the weight loss example, the All-Star may track their food preferences and calories for a week and decide on an offensive strategy of a keto diet. He/she may also switch up physical exercise to get more fat burning in. However, if an All-Star goes out to eat with friends and there are no keto options available, he/she may wait to eat, have an alternative snack, or eat the next best thing available for that one meal.

Information Synthesis

Understanding a new situation and at the same time being able to see what problems need to be solved as a result of it are traits of the All-Star. All-Stars have good focus and can pick out the things that matter in a situation, adjusting according to those things.

For example, if an All-Star wants to lose weight, he/she will look at various weight loss programs and from these options, choose the best one based on his/her personal lifestyle, needs, and goals.

Knowledge

While the All-Star will map out a plan for weight loss, if that's his/her goal, it will be based on some prior knowledge, and he/

she will be able to recall it when making an adjustment. For example, in his/her mind, he/she may go back to conversations with a doctor, knowledge of keto food availability, cost, health risks, and so on. This information will be used to decide on how to implement the diet and even when to start.

Type Two: The Maverick

Beliefs

The Maverick adjuster is a person who believes he/she can succeed and is motivated by success. Through past experiences with both success and failure, the Maverick has confidence in him/herself overall, as long as things are going well. However, if failure occurs, he/she can get emotional and be prone to self-doubt. When calm once again, the Maverick can generally regain confidence.

If a Maverick is working on losing weight and pounds are falling off per the plan, the Maverick is confident in his/her ability to succeed. But if the plan isn't working and the weight isn't coming off, the Maverick tends to experience anger, frustration, or disappointment and may lose faith in the type of weight loss plan that was chosen. He/she may even feel like he/she failed and lose faith in himself/herself. After releasing this emotion, the Maverick focuses again on success and generally returns to the original diet plan.

Timing

Internal timing for a Maverick tends to fluctuate based on his/her emotional state. This makes sense since internal timing is tied to the central nervous system and emotions can release hormones that affect the body. When a Maverick loses focus, it may take him/her a little time to calm down enough to focus well and get back to a productive timing. But once he/she does, he/she is effective. Often, a Maverick can improve timing through improving strategic actions. A Maverick with great timing will appear to have good instincts.

Strategic Actions

The Maverick is an independent thinker and wants to do well. He/she looks to strategies and tools that will help to do so, especially when failure is an option or if it feels like things are out of his/her control.

A Maverick generally operates with offensive strategies, meaning that he/she will lead initially. However, if a bump in the road happens, he/she may tend to go into defensive mode until better solutions are found and emotions calm. The Maverick improves on the offensive strategies he/she uses by not using them impulsively, rather with a little more thought. Based on this, they generally return to their original successes.

When a Maverick decides they want to lose weight they will jump right in to make it happen. Trying the newest and latest diet trend will be right up the Maverick's alley. He/she will start out strong and weight will start to come off. If the diet is trendy, it may be somewhat drastic compared to what is normal for the Maverick and somewhere in the process he/she may experience a slump. This will create frustration for the Maverick and he/she may give it up for a few weeks and look for better methods or try to understand why it doesn't work well for him/her. Later, the Maverick will come back to it and try again, this time understanding it better and succeeding.

Information Synthesis

Mavericks have good focus and can pick out the things that matter in a situation. However, they scan quickly, and it is only through difficult trials that they slow down enough to synthesize more thoroughly.

Deciding on a diet is a great example. A Maverick will look at the one that will give the best result in possibly the least amount of time. He/she will not necessarily go with what everyone else seems to be doing because he/she is motivated by success and does not always decide on the most conventional route to get there.

Knowledge

A Maverick prefers to have some knowledge and will recall prior experiences, especially when something hasn't worked out well for him/her in the past. Even though a Maverick will jump right in initially, he/she learns from the past and can recall information when it's needed so that his/her outcomes generally end up more positively.

After trying the fad diet, having some issues with it, and then returning to it, the Maverick may decide that the fad diet was too difficult overall and may not choose it in the future when trying to lose weight.

Type Three: The Mock Maverick

Beliefs

The Mock Maverick is very similar to a Maverick in belief, but the only difference is that once he/she has experienced a setback, the belief doesn't return as strongly. Even though the Mock Maverick is able to rebound like the Maverick, it is generally not the same degree of return. He/she needs to go more with their gut and not overthink their abilities. This creates doubt, even though the Mock Maverick is quite capable.

If the Mock Maverick has decided to lose weight by adding more exercise, he/she may doubt this strategy or ability if after a few weeks progress doesn't continue.

Timing

Mock Mavericks tend to give their best effort on their first stab at an adjustment, and this is also usually their best timing. They are loose when they don't feel the pressure of performance and the initial onset of a new situation or challenge is where they feel most relaxed. As the pressure mounts for the Mock Maverick, they slow down their timing in an effort not to fail. Even though they catch up in terms of adjustment, it takes them a little longer to get there.

Generally, a Mock Maverick is going to dive into the weight loss diet and take off the most weight at the beginning of his/her effort. Effort will change if there is a bump in the road but overall, the Mock Maverick will lose weight, although it might not meet the loss goal.

Strategic Actions

The Mock Maverick tends to act more from the "gut" initially. He/she will attack a new situation with an offensive strategy, but if it doesn't work out, will switch to a more defensive strategy. He/she may not switch back as quickly to an offensive strategy as a Maverick.

When a Mock Maverick has time to think through his/her strategies, he/she may feel they are not plentiful enough to adjust to new situations or challenges well. The best thing a Mock Maverick can do is to practice new strategies in order to get the confidence needed to be ready for any situation.

If the Mock Maverick's exercise plan for weight loss were to be supplemented by diet changes as well, this dual strategy would help the Mock Maverick be ready for fluctuations and not put such pressure on himself/herself to have the perfect solution right out of the gate.

Information Synthesis

Like the Maverick, the Mock Maverick scans a situation quickly but doesn't make a judgment about it until he/she has had some firsthand experience with it. From there, the Mock Maverick will look for more clues and more ways to succeed from that initial experience. Experiential information is important to the Mock Maverick and he/she will weigh that more heavily when proceeding with new ideas and strategies.

For example, if the Mock Maverick's exercise plan is too heavy in weight-lifting versus running, the Mock Maverick will know that after a short time and will change up the plan. However, as mentioned in the Strategic Actions section, the Mock Maverick may not have alternative exercise methods immediately ready to use, but he/she will try something new.

Knowledge

A Mock Maverick has an interest in learning, especially when what he/she is currently doing isn't working well. Task knowledge is more important than holistic knowledge to the Mock Maverick and they will be more interested in learning only specifically what is needed.

Type Four: The Zipper

Beliefs

The Zipper is a person who believes he/she can succeed and will attempt new things with an open mind. The Zipper is motivated by success and is not afraid of a challenge. Much like the All-Star, the Zipper will not be overly rattled by failure. In fact, he/she will tend to be more motivated by it until there is some form of success. Once they reach it, they don't stop trying but it may come in waves.

If the Zipper wants to lose weight, he/she will notice some gains in the beginning but more so as the diet continues. However, it may be the last five pounds that are the hardest for him/her.

Timing

Zippers tend to have timing differences. There are some who continue to move through an adjustment with better timing, some whose timing gets worse, and others whose timing fluctuates. However, for purposes of a strong definition, we are going to classify the true Zipper as one whose timing gets better as they move through a new or challenging situation. It's important to understand, however, that other versions of the Zipper exist. The chart at the beginning of this chapter with the section scores focuses more on the middle ground of the Zipper timing. The Signature PAR test helps to see the specifics of each individual's timing.

The true Zipper exhibits timing similar to the All-Star, but with one exception: they are not as emotionally consistent, which is why we tend to see various timing patterns in different versions.

A true Zipper will probably lose weight with a slower start then results will be seen more rapidly as they become comfortable with the plan.

Strategic Actions

The Zipper likes to have an arsenal of strategies to call upon when needed. They are naturally drawn towards offensive-type strategies similar to the All-Star. However, since they are more prone to occasional doubt, the Zipper may forget to use certain strategies or need to be reminded of ones previously learned, which could lead them to use a defensive strategy. Overall, they prefer more offensive strategies.

In the weight loss example, the Zipper will try to focus on weight loss goals that are more aggressive than those of most of their counterparts, but may find that they may need to adjust if these don't work out well.

Information Synthesis

The Zipper generally understands a situation quickly and can focus well on what needs to be done. He/she can see patterns and clues and uses that information to create effective solutions. This works well and may need to be encouraged—especially through any specific experience with failure.

For example, if a weight loss program calls for a certain food, but the Zipper doesn't have access to it, he/she will go to the store, ask someone, or go online to find a good alternative in order to continue with the diet.

Knowledge

The Zipper uses all knowledge he/she has to make good adjustments. Sometimes the breadth and depth of their knowledge can be limited due to exposure to things, but they will use what they have to succeed where they can.

Type Five: The Steady Eddy

Beliefs

The Steady Eddy is a person who believes he/she can succeed, especially with hard work. Overall, there is a positive view of their abilities. A Steady Eddy tends to be a "people-person" and is motivated by social drive as well as performance success when it comes to making adjustments.

For example, when a Steady Eddy has a goal to lose weight, he/she believes it can be done and will give a good effort. If, however, he/she goes to a restaurant with a friend, it may not be as important for the Steady Eddy to stay with the diet for that one meal. The Steady Eddy is easygoing and believes that performance can exist with camaraderie.

Timing

Interestingly enough, timing really matters with the Steady Eddy pattern. It tends to be the difference in how beliefs and strategies are applied based on how pressure is seen. Some Steady Eddys get faster with their adjustments and some get slower. However, their adjustment pattern is generally the same overall. This is where the Signature PAR test can home in on the exact nuance. External pressure is a factor in the Steady Eddy's performance.

For example, if the Steady Eddy has more confidence in a situation, he/she will tend to go faster. If he/she has less belief in success, and therefore confidence, overall timing will be slower. Confidence comes from past success in similar situations.

When losing weight, the Steady Eddy may find that how fast he/she gets results may depend on how well past attempts at losing weight have gone for him/her, barring any health changes.

If past attempts at weight loss didn't go well, the Steady Eddy may need to work on internal timing.

On question 7, if you selected that your pace of talking is faster than people around you then you most likely have the faster Steady Eddy pattern.

Strategic Actions

A Steady Eddy tends to be more evenly split between offensive and defensive strategies and may not be sure when to apply one or the other. It is found that they are pretty consistent in their adjustment actions. However, this can cause them to get stuck at times depending on how their timing plays into their adjustment abilities. If they give themselves too much time to ponder a situation, they may lose their strategy. One important thing that a Steady Eddy can do is to learn more adjustment strategies, as will be covered more in-depth later in this book.

In the weight loss example, the Steady Eddy will most likely choose a plan that has some variety in its structure, looking for what works best. He/she might also tend to prefer a workout routine that includes a class of some sort (video or in-person), a tracking app, or a coach. External ideas on how to stay on track are usually welcomed by the Steady Eddy.

Information Synthesis

A Steady Eddy may tend to get caught up in an interesting task and may not always see the big picture. Without this, the way to adjust may not be as clear at first. This can cause a more reactive rather than proactive response to a new situation. Until focus is dialed in again, the Steady Eddy may struggle with finding the patterns and clues that might be helpful in the adjustment.

Focusing only on calorie consumption for a week, for example, may lead the Steady Eddy down the road of increasing exercise, rather than pairing this information with how pants are feeling and the overall weight loss program progress.

Knowledge

Steady Eddys like what works, and they are comfortable recalling this information to inform their adjustments. Steady Eddys who tend to get faster in multiple attempts at adjustments tend to enjoy learning more than those who do not get faster. Those who don't will need encouragement and a good learning plan.

Type Six: The Mascot

Beliefs

The Mascot believes he/she can succeed and has a positive view of his/her abilities, as long as he/she feels that the adjustment is necessary and will have a positive impact on his/her life. Mascots tend to fear change, failure, or loss of control.

When a Mascot has a goal to lose weight, he/she believes it can be done and will give a good effort—but only when he/she is ready and believes the plan is worth doing. If someone pushes the plan on a Mascot, he/she may be less motivated to attempt it. Living up to someone else's expectations or ideas of progress isn't something that is attractive to the Mascot.

Timing

The Mascot may initially take his/her time to attack a new situation, but then once he/she has made some impressions about it, internal timing speeds up. This may be due to the patience or belief regarding the situation, deciding that it may not be worth investing much time into. Patience and effort require energy, and the Mascot is particular about where he/she chooses to spend it.

If a Mascot decides to start on a weight loss plan, and it requires significant energy, the Mascot may attempt it but then abandon the plan after a short time. The "why" behind starting the weight loss program to begin with would be important for the Mascot in determining how long he/she will stay with it.

Strategic Actions

A Mascot tends to be more rooted in defensive strategies than offensive ones. He/she will use the best defensive strategies, especially when offensive ones aren't working. Multiple strategies are not always a strong trait of the Mascot. Learning more about various strategies would be a good way for the Mascot to improve his/her adjustment ability.

For the Mascot to lose weight, a program that is already clearly laid out with specific expectations and anticipated loss results is key.

Information Synthesis

The Mascot scans a new situation and looks for information that aligns with or is inconsistent with his/her beliefs about the new situation. Information regarding whether the potential outcome requires significant effort will be taken into account strongest when attempting something new. In addition, the Mascot may not always look for new patterns in any given information.

A Mascot will look at a weight loss program to evaluate if it requires significant changes to his/her routine, and this will influence his/her decision regarding whether to implement it or not.

Knowledge

Knowledge is important to a Mascot, and he/she applies learned knowledge to new situations. In fact, sometimes that knowledge is what drives him/her to make quick judgments about whether to engage in performance adjustment.

Type Seven: The Free Agent

Beliefs

The Free Agent isn't quite sure if he/she can succeed. This is true in new situations or when he/she doesn't think an adjustment will make a significant difference. In addition, Free Agents will tend to pull back on their motivation if they can't see an immediate payoff to their effort or they are afraid of revealing their own self-doubt. The Free Agent is motivated by protecting self-comfort and self-image and will steer clear of situations where this can be challenged.

If a Free Agent wants to lose weight, he/she may try a diet for a few days but then give up on it when progress doesn't come quickly enough in order to protect himself/herself from feeling like a "failure."

Timing

When a Free Agent decides that a new situation might be too difficult for him/her, the pressure that they internally create is so great that it causes their timing to either be very quick or very slow. Of course, this is a reaction to what the Free Agent believes he/she is capable of and how much he/she is willing to try. Overall effort may be disrupted, and therefore, timing will be too.

If a Free Agent is on a diet, they need quick results in order to stay engaged with it.

Strategic Actions

A Free Agent uses mostly defensive strategies when working through something new and uncertain or after some form of loss or failure. This is due in large part to the fact that the Free Agent has not gained the confidence to employ more offensive strategies and may not be familiar with how to use them well.

In order for the Free Agent to lose weight, he/she has to have great confidence in a program's effectiveness and outcomes. Losing weight is an offensive-type activity by nature (if it is by choice), meaning that it is initiated by the person who wants it to happen. Therefore, it will require the defensive-thinking Free Agent to move out of his/her comfort zone in order for it to happen.

Information Synthesis

The Free Agent is similar to the Mascot when it comes to information synthesis. He/she will also scan a new situation and looks to see whether or not the potential outcome requires significant effort. However, the Free Agent will also look for information that might shed light as to what additional pressure would be involved in the situation.

If the weight loss program requires the Free Agent to compare his/her results with others who are in the program, he/she will look to see how that is done and decide if this is the program for them. If it is done anonymously or very positively, the Free Agent may feel more comfortable with this and go forward.

Knowledge

The Free Agent is interested in knowledge but may not always know how to apply it in high-pressure situations. Our bodies release hormones, like cortisol, when we are in stressful situations. Cortisol tends to "close the door" to our brain so that we can react. This is a survival mechanism. However, when we need to access information, we can't do this easily when under threat. This could be one reason the Free Agent struggles with accessing information and memory in new and uncertain situations.

Scoring the knowledge tendencies of the Free Agent tends to be straightforward. The reason is that they do value knowledge; they just can't always access it when it's needed.

What If I Have More Than One Pattern Tendency?

By now you have an idea of where your basic five adjustment tendencies fit under the seven natural adjustment types. Maybe your scores showed that your tendencies fit under more than one adjustment type. This is very normal due to the language and culture bias in a paper-based test, and why the Signature PAR test itself is the main tool for actual pattern discernment. However, the AAA will get you close enough to understand your basic pattern tendencies.

As mentioned earlier in this chapter, we have, on occasion, seen "combination" pattern types, especially in clustering data exercises. As this research continues, we see the increased importance of timing on pattern types, which makes sense with the increase in automation and digital transformation that is occurring globally.

Maybe after reading about your tendencies, you aren't happy with the outcome of the audit and are hoping for a little direction on what to do to improve it. Or, maybe you feel good about your tendencies but want to know more about how to grow or help others. Learning how to make tweaks to these tendencies is one of the best things you can do to train your adjustment muscle to grow, improve, and be ready for any change or uncertainty that comes your way.

CHAPTER 6

Making Better Adjustments

"Some people dream of success while others wake up
and work hard at it."

—UNKNOWN

Baseball was my second career. I didn't start working in base-ball until my kids were in late grade school, and I was on the cusp of forty. My first, shorter career was in corporate America. I soon learned that college and the real world didn't always line up. The corporate world required new adjustments. Immediately, I was signed up for professional development training, where I had to learn things that I wasn't taught in college, such as the ins and outs of business etiquette, digital skills, quality, team building, and so on.

Many years later, when I started working in baseball, I realized quickly that I had stepped into another world yet again. This was truly a "people" business, and skills were a given. Your results had to speak for themselves. There was pressure, but it was a different kind of pressure. It surprised me often. For example, the first time I witnessed a "goodbye baseball" speech, as I call it, it was a shocker.

I was in the classroom when the Latin liaison of the team, "Chuey" as he was nicknamed, came in to observe the class. It happened to be in mid-July, when the players were worn out and tired. They had had a doubleheader the day before, and the energy was a little low. The international players who were plopped in a Midwest affiliate always struggled the most starting in July. They were feeling homesick and, of course, tired from the daily play.

Chuey noticed right away that the players were low on energy, so he decided to jump in and give them a motivational talk. He told them in Spanish that being able to learn new skills was a huge opportunity for them. He said that as a player himself, he wished he would have had these opportunities. Then he said, "Baseball is not forever. It ends someday for everyone. Take every opportunity you can today to make it last as long as you can." I never heard anyone say anything remotely close to that in corporate America! You only hear this when you're on a sports team, especially at the college and pro levels. This speech wasn't meant to hurt or embarrass them but to help them realize the importance of time and effort. It was an honest reality check from one who had been in their shoes. Since this speech, Chuey has spoken in high schools and to many others in sports. He is a gifted coach and speaker.

The players immediately responded to this and pulled out whatever energy they had left to make it a great class. They realized that every day matters and that they needed to rise up and apply themselves in order to be their best. Regrets are stones, tied to your waist, that drag behind you. No one needs that kind of weight!

I thought about how this honesty is so different than what is being taught today. Can you imagine your boss telling you that someday your job will end, never knowing exactly when that day is? How about your spouse? "Hey, honey, take every opportunity to be a good spouse because someday this is going to end." *What?!*

We don't plan on being "cut" from our work, relationships, or our lives. But knowing how to adjust to an unexpected circumstance, change, failure, or even opportunity is a skill that will help us continue to respect every day for what it brings and not take it for granted. In addition, we can be at peace knowing that we did our best at the time.

The Adjustment Skill Set

Knowing how to make a great adjustment is, in itself, a skill set. It is something that we talk about and toss around all the time, but we don't realize that it has to be learned. Can you imagine someone saying something to you like, "Just do some surgery, and things will get better"? But it isn't that easy, is it? Isn't that what we say about adjustment? "Look, just make an adjustment, and things will get better." I realize that performing surgery is far more complicated, but you get the idea. We need some training to perform surgery, and we need some training to make good adjustments.

If we go back to the five elements of adjustments (belief, strategic actions, timing, information synthesis, and knowledge), isolate and start training them, we can begin to see improvements in performance, goal-reaching, and overall peace. When I have worked with people on isolating and training adjustment skills, I have seen a roughly 20 percent to 30 percent average improvement in their performance quite quickly. It's simply a matter of optimizing what we already have. Whether you are an MLB pitcher, an up-and-coming sales manager, an online entrepreneur, or a person with any goal, performance adjustment skills transform your self-awareness into big-league action.

If I were going to work with you on training your "adjustment" muscle, I would ask you a few questions like, "What are your beliefs about adjustment in general?" and "What goal are you aiming for?" and "What does your timing look like?" These questions would help me establish your motivation. You can never escape the need in your life to adjust—it is part of living. My hope is that your motivation would be to want to live a better, more productive life and be prepared for whatever the future might hold in store for you without anxiety.

Assuming you are motivated, let's look at some simple ways that adjustment skills can be trained.

Tick Tock and Rock It

Our internal clocks shape the way we perceive time, rhythm, and coordination. These internal clocks are largely controlled by our brain pulses, carried by the nervous system, and the patterns of behavior we develop over time. These patterns impact how well we focus during times of change, uncertainty, or failure.

When I work with an individual or an organization on adjustment training, one of the first things I do is explain natural timing. Once we know our natural, internal timing, we can begin to see the differences and where they tend to fit together. Interestingly enough, people who have similar timing traits tend to be found in similar job roles/positions.

To find your natural timing, go to any metronome application online. A metronome is a device that marks time at a selected rate by a ticking noise. If you play music or know someone who does, you may have seen the old-style wooden metronome. Today, there are digital versions of these online. Basically, it is a device that makes an audible ticking sound, which can be made to go faster or slower.

A "baseline" timing is important to know. This is the rate at which we feel the most comfortable at rest, not engaged in anything with high levels of possible stress. In other words, it's the rate at which we are *not* paying much attention to anything else, just the audible beat of time. When we start to pay attention to other things, we are no longer paying attention to the beat of time alone. However, this is the reality of life, and we can't walk around only paying attention to our internal timing.

We are made to pay attention to the things that impact survival first. Food, shelter, love, and such are the things we more easily focus on. But in today's society, we are being bombarded by grabs for our attention. This is causing confusion, paralysis, and a lack of joy.

It is inevitable that, at times, we need to split our focus. This is true, especially in sports. But if we can allow ourselves to focus only on internal timing for awareness and training, we can begin to see how it shapes our day. The truth is that our relationship with time determines how we expend energy. This is why knowing your baseline is important.

Once we find our comfortable baseline timing, we can start adding in simple tasks that take our concentration. I use a variety of activities from easy thinking (prefrontal cortex activation) to more difficult. You could do the same thing as well. With the comfortable rhythm in the background, all tasks should be done to that rhythm.

When that is comfortable, you can speed up the timing a little at a time and increase the complexity of the activities. I look for both speed and accuracy to the goal. The activities should always change so that "memorization" is not possible.

The final stage of this type of adjustment training is to apply this to a task that you are interested in succeeding at. For example, let's look at how we could apply this to weight loss.

One way to apply internal timing training is to focus on the weight loss process that you generally don't do well. For the sake of an example, let's say it is preparing meals ahead of time. If we were going to train your internal timing to concentrate on this, we would use it as part of the training. We might bring in a series of pictures of prepped meals that would be flipped through to the increasing rhythm in the background.

By doing this, you concentrate on this task, and when you pair it with concentrating on internal rhythms at the same time, you etch it stronger into your brain. Concentration has its limits, and learning how to stay focused (or "locked in") while making adjustments is a big part of making successful ones.

If your goal is to get better at a work task, you could use this same idea. Try working to your natural rhythm. Then slowly start increasing the audible timing to where you feel you reach your task limit. These time-based activities will increase your concentration. Holding concentration for longer periods or several weeks, months, or even years in order to accomplish a goal is a true skill.

Training internal timing is one part of improving your adjustment muscle. There are two more areas that will immediately impact it as well: Strategic Actions and Information Synthesis. The other two, beliefs and knowledge, are much more complicated and are not discussed in this book. However, let's look at strategic actions, one element that can be trained a little easier to see immediate adjustment improvement.

Checkmate

In any sport, most players and coaches know about two main types of strategies: offense and defense. An offensive strategy is one where a person or group of people try to actively score a point for their team. A defensive strategy is one where a person or group of people try to defend their position and stop the competition from scoring. If you've ever played on a sports team, most likely you've been part of the offense or defense. Offensive strategy can be equated to playing to win. A defensive strategy is playing not to lose.

While having the two broad offense and defense categories is important, there are a few more options within each one. Let's take a look at the most common types of strategies within the categories.

Offensive Strategies

In general, offensive strategies give us control, and for some people, that feels a little uncomfortable. Why? There is more risk. This can cause fear and paralysis. However, without employing offensive strategies on occasion, it is more difficult to reach goals and improve performance. The beauty of focusing on adjustment is that if an offensive strategy didn't work perfectly in the past, it can be adjusted. We don't have to feel stuck.

There are various offensive strategies used in war, business, and sports. But the two that I want to focus on are called direct and preemptive.

DIRECT

Direct offense is one of the most aggressive strategies. It is likened to a type of competitive "attack" on the defense. This type of strategy has a specific outcome in mind and will mean extra energy and resources are spent up front to accomplish this goal. Digital transformation in America is a great example of a direct offense because when it is adopted by a corporation, everyone has to learn how to use it. It becomes part of the "norm."

For job seekers, reaching out and asking owners about job openings is also a great example of an offensive strategy. A direct offense might be to offer to work for free for a given time so that the employer can see the skill set, drive, and determination a person brings to the organization. Large corporations might not be able to take advantage of this, but small to mid-size ones can. Oftentimes small steps lead to bigger opportunities.

PREEMPTIVE

A preemptive offensive strategy is a little different than a direct offense. It means to be the first one "there," or in the seat of advantage. It may not be as aggressive as the direct offense, but it is one step ahead of the crowd in a way that makes it difficult to "unseat" someone who is already there. Innovative ideas and strong implementation plans are part of the preemptive strategy. When the new app, Clubhouse, started, people were trying to be the first to be the "go-to" person in a certain area of expertise in order to gain a large following, which could be used to leverage products or services. This is a preemptive offensive strategy.

After reviewing the results from the Signature PAR test, it is easy to see if the test taker is operating from a vantage point of an offensive or defensive strategy.

Defensive Strategies

Defensive strategies are more reactive, countering moves made by the offense. Interestingly enough, many people feel more comfortable in the defensive position. In fact, I find that approximately 60 percent of the people I test feel this way. Fear has really entered into the adjustment equation, and I believe it's due to things like cancel culture and an intense focus on safety. It's much easier to wait and watch than to run and do. In my opinion, this is unfortunate for the strength of America overall.

However, we need defensive strategies in addition to offensive ones in order to make great adjustments. The reason is that sometimes an offensive move isn't the best one at the time, and employing a defensive move can set us up for when the time is right to act. The decision-making part of our brain, or prefrontal cortex, has work to do when deciding which strategy to employ. Often it will lean on a few of the other elements to make this decision.

While there are various defensive strategies used in war, business, and sports, the two that most directly impact adjustments are called counter-parry and blocking.

COUNTER-PARRY

Counter-parry is a more aggressive defensive strategy that puts the offense in a slightly awkward position. The idea is to counter what the offense does with something strong. If you've ever watched a boxing or fencing match, you have probably witnessed counter-parry moves.

Working in a man's world, especially in pro sports, I was often in need of a good defensive strategy. I never knew when a joking jab would come my way, and after a few failed attempts at rebuttals, I knew I had to make an adjustment in this area. Eventually, I became effective in the verbal counter-parry, not too aggressive nor too submissive. Through this defensive strategy, I was able to move past the doubts of my aggressors and stand my ground. I had to learn this strategy and when to use it, which took some practice but turned out to be very effective—especially when tied with great timing.

BLOCKING

A blocking defense is used to block out, or deflect, an offensive move. It isn't as powerful as a counter-parry but allows some time for the defender to reset in some way. You may be wondering how this very sports-like idea relates to everyday adjustments. Defensive actions are not just against competitors; they are part of our everyday situations.

For example, I have seen international players use humor as a very effective blocking defense. When teased by a teammate, they smile, laugh, and "block" the attack through submissive avoidance. Learning and practicing offensive and defensive strategies are important parts of adjustment skills.

Filters On!

Information is always coming at us in various ways—both directly and indirectly. Things like sound, sight, and touch tell us many things about our environment. We receive information through all of our senses, and we try to break it down and make it meaningful. This is a skill that isn't talked about much but is very important to good adjustments. There are many resources on the internet that give ideas about how to become a better "synthesizer," but they mostly relate to music or writing skills. Making good adjustments calls for a slightly modified version of information synthesis.

Synthesizing information to make good adjustments requires four basic things: scanning, comparing, deciding, and creating.

Scanning involves paying attention to your goal and the information in front of you that can help you reach that goal. For example, if your goal is to lose weight, what foods do you have in your kitchen now?

Comparing means looking at what you already know against what you have in front of you. In the case of losing weight, you might look to see what foods in your kitchen right now are important to helping you reach your goal and which ones aren't.

Deciding and creating go hand in hand. Sometimes it is simply a matter of determining the best course of action based on the scanning and comparing that you just did. Other times it's creating a new situation. For example, if all of the food in your kitchen isn't going to move you closer to weight loss, then it's time to get new food. By doing so, you created a new option. In addition, you used an offensive strategy!

When I am training a person to improve information synthesis skills, I may put visuals in front of him/her and ask that person to scan for specific things. This can be auditory information as well. The key is to know specifically what you are trying to improve upon and focus the information only around that one item. This means you have to know what matters. You're not scanning for everything because this would be information overload. You are intentional about what you are scanning for. Practicing this skill means identifying something in your goal that you need to focus on and looking for it in the situations that you could find it in.

Once a person can pick out the correct information, I ask him/her to compare it against what he/she is doing right now and identify how it is different. You could do the same thing with your own goal in mind. Finally, the person has to decide which piece of information will be most useful in performance and we talk about how it can be applied. This usually involves some further activities using the beat of time or some other means to increase speed, as in the internal timing examples from the earlier section.

But it doesn't stop with this. Information synthesis is ongoing, and that means that it is happening all the time. The reason is that things are always changing, so we always need great information and the ability to filter it in order to decide our next steps. Many people will do this cycle once, maybe twice, and make almost all future decisions based on these few times. Great adjusters are always scanning for new information against their goals, filtering it, and finding new ways to improve performance based on it.

The Elements Cocktail

The Signature PAR test helped us uncover and show players what they weren't seeing in the way they made adjustments: their "blind spot," so to speak. As you read about your tendencies from the AAA, did you see some things that surprised you? We all have blind spots, and we need a mirror to show us ours.

I have found that strengthening the blind spot usually impacts other pattern areas as well. That means we have to know how the elements work together, and exactly what their individual contributions were. Much of the time, I found that it was dependent on what the end goal was. For example, if the goal in baseball was to improve a specific offensive- or defensive-related statistic, we would test to see where exactly adjustment skills needed improving.

For example, I worked with a pitcher who was showing inconsistencies and letting hitters get on base. After looking at his PAR

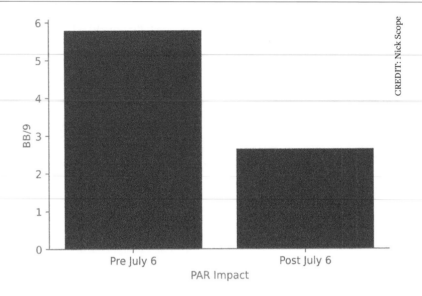

CREDIT: Nick Scope

test and tracking the way he made adjustments, I was able to find the weakness and help him improve it. Here is an example of statistical information regarding this player's performance before and after making adjustments:

You can clearly see that after working on his adjustment pattern deficiencies, the player lowered this statistic by more than half, which was what we were going for. This was very motivating for him. He dominated the rest of the year and was promoted quickly to the next level. However, every level will bring new adjustments. The work is ongoing. Smart players know that.

When training adjustment skills, it is important to recognize that each element has a "potency," and when mixed with the others, it may lose some of its original strength depending on outcomes. Let's see how this works.

Let's imagine you just experienced an obstacle, or a disruptor, on the road to achieving a goal. Your adjustment skills will kick into play, but each element will get involved in a different way, depending on your past experience and each effort you give going forward. The potency levels of each adjustment element can change depending on the situation duration and frequency.

For example's sake, let's look at potency upon our first encounter with this disruptor.

Element Potency

Upon our first encounter with an obstacle, we all sift through various questions in our minds in order to tackle it. In doing so, certain types of information will be placed at higher importance and priority, depending on the number of times we see this obstacle. If we see an obstacle for the first time, the order will be different than if we have seen that obstacle and its outcomes two or three times before.

For example, Sarah works as a nurse in the hospital, and she gets a new patient with a virus she hasn't seen before. When she realizes that this is a new condition, she will run through thoughts in her mind, and in a certain order. This tends to be the order of the elements on the first encounter:

#1 Information Synthesis

The first questions Sarah asks are, "What is this?" and, "Have I seen this before?" She will look for familiar patterns to give her some information on how to proceed. This includes asking the patient questions, asking other nurses and doctors for information, and consulting medical records.

#2 Knowledge

In addition to patterns, we look for a memory of an obstacle like this that we may have encountered in the past. We try to pull from our experience and any information we may have in order to work through this obstacle. In Sarah's case, she may ask, "Do I know what to do?" and, "What did I do in the past when I saw something like this?"

#3 Strategic Action

After we size up what we know, the next question would look something like this: "What steps do I need to take to succeed?" or, "Should I attack this aggressively or more passively?" Sarah would most likely take a more conservative approach, depending on the danger of the new virus on the patient.

#4 Internal Timing

If we have the steps and are willing to take them, now we ask, "How much time will this take now and how long will I be at it overall?" or, "Will I have to speed up or slow down my normal rate of effort?" If the patient seems to be doing fine, Sarah may not speed up her actions because she feels no stress. But if the patient is not doing well, she will most likely speed up the treatment plan.

#5 Belief

Assuming we have some idea on how to proceed based on the prior questions, we now ask, "Do I think I can conquer this?" or, "How strong is my doubt/fear?" or, "Does this align with my faith?" In Sarah's case, since someone else's life is in danger, she may need to rely not only on her own beliefs but also on those of her team in order to figure this out and help the patient.

Second encounter, same obstacle

If we see this same obstacle again, our adjustment elements may change order and potency. For example, let's say a second patient with the same lethal virus comes into Sarah's hospital, and she is the nurse for that patient. The elements and their priority will shift depending on what the outcome of Sarah's first encounter was. For the sake of the example, let's say that, unfortunately, the first patient did not survive. I choose this worst-case scenario because it will allow you to see a more typical shift in the elements.

#1 Belief

If our first attempt at something did not succeed, it is easier to doubt ourselves, our skills, and our ability to succeed. Now doubt and fear may be stronger.

#2 Strategic Action

Knowing the first patient died and this second patient is in danger, Sarah would most likely take more aggressive action depending on what the patient can tolerate.

#3 Internal Timing

The normal rate of effort will automatically change based on the complexity of the obstacle. It will either slow down or speed up, depending on how much doubt and fear are influencing it.

#4 & #5 Information Synthesis/Knowledge

The knowledge and memory of that first attempt will now be very strong when deciding how to move forward, and that may even be part of synthesizing new information.

However, all proper information may not be synthesized depending on how strong the emotion becomes and the timing requirements.

Notice how the elements almost reversed order after a failed attempt at performance in a high-stakes situation. This isn't always the case, but it is the most typical according to our findings on adjustment patterns. In addition, I have found that we can influence order somewhat based on what happens *before* the situation is turned over to the person to resolve it.

The key here is that the more attempts at a similar performance, the more our pattern becomes ingrained. That's why it is important to be aware of it and find ways to train the areas that are causing us to repeat failure. You can see how transformative this can be when it comes to learning, growth, and performance.

The Adjustment Skill Set

Learning how to improve your adjustment skills takes some practice, and that's why the adjustment program that comes after the Signature PAR test has been a crucial part of my work. Just knowing that you can train yourself to make better adjustments has been a game-changer for many people. You don't have to stay stuck in the same patterns, and you do have options to adjust more calmly and intentionally. When new situations or change comes your way, if you focus on the five elements of adjustment outlined in chapter 2, the results from your AAA, and the ideas in this chapter, you will start to see a better plan of attack evolve, which will positively impact your life.

Over the years, I have seen various types of adjusters. I have had many people ask me what a "good" pattern is and what a "bad" pattern is. While most patterns have some areas that need optimizing, even if ever so slightly, some patterns come my way every so often that make me sit back and think, "Wow." These are individuals that I call million dollar adjusters.

Who are these people? What do they do differently, and why should that matter? Turn the page!

CHAPTER 7

The Traits of a
Million Dollar Adjuster

"Baseball is 90 percent mental and the other half is physical."

—YOGI BERRA

How We Do Everything

Years ago, I heard the phrase, "How we do anything is how we do everything." In other words, we have underlying patterns that operate quietly in the background of our lives. We may not always recognize them, but the people closest to us generally can. If you think about it, do you think your family or close friends can predict how you might do something? How do they know that? Through spending time with you, they have seen your patterns and can recognize their influence in your decision-making, activities, thresholds of change, and execution of tasks. You can probably see the same in them.

Your preferences, efforts, physical growth, and even your language skills have all been subject to some types of adjustments throughout your life. These adjustments fine-tune your success in life and lead you to activate your innate gifts and abilities in some way.

By peeking into how a person makes an adjustment, it became clear that how you do anything is truly how you do everything, unless, of course, you train it differently. But first, you have to know "how you do anything." This a broad statement because there are various factors at play. For us, we were looking at how a person currently adjusts to new or changing tasks, situations, pressures, and even failures. We were not looking at aptitudes, intelligence, or personality. That's not the "anything" we were focusing on. There are plenty of assessments that do this already. The Signature PAR assessment was developed to help us see how adjustments are made under stressful, uncertain, and failure-based situations. These conditions express variables that no other test can render, and that is the "anything" we were interested in. Since failure is a possibility in almost anything we do, we had to have that piece built in.

The next step was to see if "how you do everything" would show up too. In baseball, everything is playing games. We decided to run PAR data against on-field data models to see how they compared. This was a little tricky because there are many months of data throughout a baseball season, as there would be in life, and we had to decide which data to clean and use. We made some assumptions and chose specific on-field performance statistics relative to position and in the timeframe that made the most sense to a baseball organization. We ran the models and saw that many of the statistics aligned. It was astounding to see the mathematical significance! PAR lined up over 70 percent of the time with on-field performance. Here is an example from some of our initial modeling:

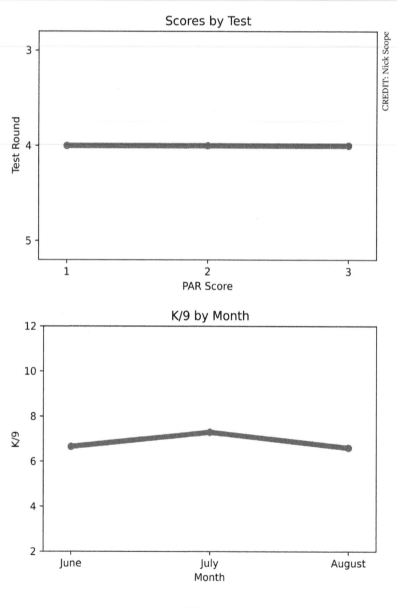

In both of these graphs, you will notice a line in the middle running from left to right. The line on the left is straight, and the line on the right has a little incline in the middle. You can clearly see that both lines are very similar, with just a slight difference. The graph on the left shows a person's results from the PAR test, and the picture on the right shows on-field performance in one area.

This means that if a pitcher was tested and found to have a flat PAR score, he made relatively few adjustments and stayed constant in most things—like the Steady Eddy. It also means that he most likely performed that way on the field, which is what the picture on the right shows. The K/9 statistic means strike-outs per nine innings, which is one indicator of how a pitcher is doing in a game. It's very significant to see both of these lines looking almost identical. In order to truly change the K/9, the PAR elements need to be optimized in this area.

New School Metrics

Just like the graphs above, over and over again, we saw similar correlations, and I felt confident that this information could be used in the classroom to help players learn. By knowing an individual player's adjustment pattern, I could train the weak areas and create new learning methods to maximize the traits I saw beginning to emerge in these patterns. Wouldn't you love it if a teacher did that for you or your child? As a mom, I knew I was serving the players the best I could by doing this for them.

Through this shift in teaching, new metrics to help measure progress were being generated. I was beginning to see which adjustment types were learning faster than others and why. The five adjustment elements will be potent in various combinations depending on the number of experiences a person has within a situation. I started to keep track of situational frequency and how the elements responded, reinforcing element strength and order rather than focusing solely on traditional learning success metrics. When the constrained element was isolated and optimized, if it was seen positively affecting the other elements, I considered that progress and included it as a percentage in the overall "grade." I called this the EIM, or Element Impact Matrix.

If you remember, in chapter 4, "dumbos" were considered the players who couldn't learn or who had few schooling opportunities. The reason I didn't see that in the classroom is that it wasn't about intelligence or special opportunities. It was more about adjustment skills. It made sense. Without these skills, anything and everything is more difficult. With these skills, learning is fun. For players, school was suddenly cool, or "dope!"

Of course, on occasion, there would be players with special circumstances that slowed learning, even with adjustment skills training and the EIM system. Things like medical issues and emotional trauma that required more specific interventions were outside of the impact of the learning system. However, players who weren't experiencing these things showed enhanced learning and renewed engagement with the classroom curriculum.

The Amateur Draft

One day, while in a routine meeting with associates in player development, I was asked about player language progress. I pulled out my data and began to share some insights in ways that the team had never heard. Little did I know that one of the people in that meeting was also working with the scouting department. Suddenly, I was asked to share more about the PAR and its correlations with the executive baseball operations team.

A meeting was scheduled, and I traveled to the team's administrative offices. I presented the background on the test, a general idea of data patterns and trends as well as what it was showing us about on-field performance. This team had a research and development department and was already using advanced player technology techniques, but there was still something missing. How could they know if someone would progress and learn after he/she was signed? This is important because they signed players to the team before they developed into major-league players. This is why the minor league is considered a development league. The staff there is trying to develop them to be in the major league.

This meeting led to a series of follow-up conversations, and the next thing I knew, I was traveling around the country, testing players for the amateur draft. The idea was to get just a little more information regarding how a player might develop and how long it might take.

Have you ever heard the phrase, "information is power?" This phrase implies that when we have the right information at the right time, we can make better decisions and possibly take big actions. Without information, improvement efforts are more difficult. This is why big corporations keep metrics: to monitor their systems and make adjustments when things are going off track. With market information, they can also take advantage of emerging opportunities. Information gives them the ability to lower risk or increase opportunity.

When a professional baseball team is about to invest millions of dollars to sign a player, there is risk for the team. They spend a lot of time gathering information on a player in order to make a proper decision on what to offer him. Everything is used to evaluate performance potential because young players are usually signed for projected future value. It isn't an easy equation. Player talent is important, but so is "make-up." This is a term to describe a player's mental capacities, character, personality, aptitudes, and all things nonphysical. It was kind of a catchall for anything above the neck. It took an experienced baseball scout to know what was considered a good make-up versus a bad one, and even then, sometimes they were wrong. Although Major League Baseball had some guidelines, many teams still had their own ways of getting this type of information. It wasn't easy and took a lot of discussion. If you've ever seen the movie *Moneyball*, there is a scene showing scouts around a table talking about players. This was attempting to show this process.

Imagine you were the one responsible for making these big decisions. What would you want to know about a player? This person not only has to play well but will be interacting and traveling with the team and be around coaches, trainers, dieticians, and so on every day. I'm sure you would be interested in knowing about "make-up" too.

Million Dollar Adjusters

Over the years, I tested thousands of players. It was fun to hear the names of players I had the opportunity to test be called in the draft. I knew this was the first step of many. Post-test and post-draft, my team and I followed player careers to see which patterns seemed to thrive. After collecting and analyzing test data, it became clear that certain traits and patterns did better over the long haul as well as the baseline ones that were needed to "get in the door." While all players who made it from the minor leagues to the major leagues were great adjusters, I called an even more select few million dollar adjusters (or MDAs for short), because they had a certain "something else," success DNA, if you will, that went beyond my baseline metrics, great work ethic, and talent.

I call these million dollar traits, because this smaller, elite group had strong performance success rates, staying power, and higher salaries. In summarizing this data in a way that makes sense to the reader, I found it easier to provide what made them distinct, traits shared by almost all MDAs. I'm sure I would have missed it if we weren't actually tracking each adjustment, rather than looking at results overall. It's amazing what we find out when we track our adjustments, in addition to looking at the overall outcome.

I believe that we can all find something in these traits that can apply to our lives in whatever game we're playing.

Trait #1 Million Dollar Adjusters are Decisive

When faced with a new situation, a million dollar adjuster will make a decision in order to move forward. He doesn't spend time waiting for all the information or for someone to tell him what to do. He scans the information he has and takes the best action he can at the time. This requires effective processing speed and cognitive control. If his initial actions are not fruitful, he will scan again and decide on the next, subsequent action. The ability to be decisive requires cognitive flexibility and higher levels of belief because, in most situations, it is virtually impossible to have all the information needed to make perfect decisions all the time. A million dollar adjuster accepts this fact and believes in successful outcomes regardless of the information that is missing.

Trait #2 Million Dollar Adjusters Maximize Time

A million dollar adjuster is in tune with his timing and is inherently able to control his emotions, which helps sustain positive energy through tasks he is working on. Normal emotions like frustration or anxiety do not create a big enough impact to shut down or alter his timing. He practices patience when working through new situations, not cutting corners just to get through it or allowing pressure to overtake his natural timing.

Maximizing time is also valuing time, no matter what the situation. When time is taken for granted, important things can be missed. Million dollar adjusters value time in ways that most others do not.

Trait #3 Million Dollar Adjusters Can Sustain Attention After Failure

Our test data shows that MDAs are not easily distracted and can focus well for a continuous amount of time, even after a failed task. Once a million dollar adjuster makes a decision, sustained attention allows him to follow through on it. An MDA can keep their attention from shifting to irrelevant activities and instead focus on the task at hand, even if new events occur, such as failure or uncertain outcomes. When failures do occur, million dollar adjusters don't make that part of their identity. They know their value in a different way than their counterparts.

Trait #4 Million Dollar Adjusters See Solutions and Relevant Correlations

By being able to sustain attention, MDAs see solutions that others might miss. They activate their memory and cognitive flexibility in order to continually make improvements. To them, all small gains matter because they are part of a bigger solution. An MDA will embrace learning in order to increase knowledge, apply it, and get closer to a goal. In addition, while growing new solutions, an MDA will, at the same time, recycle and perfect strategies that have proven to be effective in the past. This, of course, requires some previous memory of what worked and why.

If you look closely at these four traits, you will see something familiar. The five basic elements of adjustment are here, setting the foundation for something greater. In fact, it was in analyzing the patterns and the tracking data that we started to see the basic five. It was in varying degrees, but they were all there in some form. A million dollar adjuster knows how to use these five elements well.

The following graphs show the Signature PAR test results of two major league players. This first one shows an infield player who was chosen in the late round of the amateur draft, with a signing bonus of $50,000. If you're familiar with baseball, that's not a big bonus. However, today he is a million dollar adjuster, and his salary reflects that. His test score looks like the chart on the following page.

This player exhibits the four qualities of a million dollar adjuster. If you look at the top line, you will notice that it trends downward. The closer this gets to one, the better. You can see that his trending is going in that direction. This means he is a person who tends to make improvements overall, which is a direct reflection of traits 3 and 4. To improve, a person has to be able to see solutions (strategic actions, information synthesis, and knowledge). Seeing solutions is not possible without sustained attention.

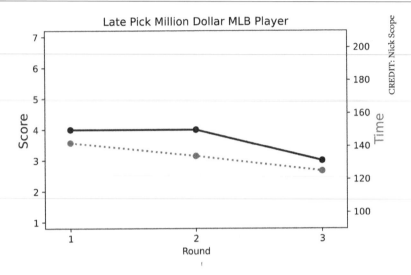

The bottom dotted line shows the player's timing and how it improves as well. It consistently goes down, showing that improvement isn't taking more time but less. Do you see traits 1 and 2? A downward trend means that time is maximized through quick action (belief and timing). This can't be done with a head full of doubts. There has to be confidence that comes from someplace. Where does it come from? It comes from trust. Trust happens through mindset, methods, and wisdom gained from weighing decisions well and being ever on the lookout for a false sense of security. Success isn't security or stability. Failure isn't forever. Million dollar adjusters understand the in-between and don't doubt either condition.

Now let's look at another example. This graph shows the Signature PAR test results of another early draft pick who made it to the major leagues. His signing bonus was $950,000 (nineteen times the amount given to the player above!). However, his salary never reached that of a million dollar adjuster, nor did his longevity. He is no longer playing in Major League Baseball.

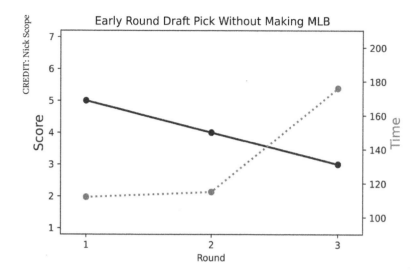

CREDIT: Nick Scope

What happened here? This was an early draft pick! If we look at his top line score, it trends downward, just like the top player, which is good. So far, it looks like he is able to master the first trait, decisiveness. It also seems that he has the fourth trait, seeing solutions and relevant correlations. Hmmm, so far, so good.

Now let's look at the lower dotted line, which represents time. Notice the first dot at the beginning of that line and how far apart it is from the top line. What does this say? It says that the thinking was impulsive. This is not a good use of time. In fact, time didn't seem to be valued; the player hurried through the task. As you look at the second and third dot along the lower line, do you see that it continually goes up? This means that failure is causing emotions to soar and the player can't sustain attention. Now the player isn't so decisive because it is taking longer. One could argue that he is getting better, and that is true. Sometimes it takes us longer to get better, and that's a perfectly good thing.

But these are developmental steps that should have happened in the minor leagues and not in the major leagues. Someone pushed this player too soon, and he didn't have the adjustment skills to compete at the highest levels. Unless there is some intervention and adjustment skills development, this player will suffer from this experience. This is more common than one might think, which is why we don't see many million dollar adjusters.

Your Million Dollar Adjustment

Perhaps after looking at these charts and reading about these elite traits, you may be wondering how you can use this information in a practical way. You probably have no plans of trying out for the major leagues of baseball or any sport, yet you have your own million dollar adjustment going on in your life. This could be anything important to you, whether it is financial freedom, more joy in your life, a new business, or to just lose a few pounds. You can do any of these things because you can adjust to the ups and downs of success and failure. You see that even elite performers have ups and downs, and yet, they don't stop. They have mastered the art of adjustment, and you can too.

In the last chapter, you learned some ways to help train your adjustment skill set. You may have looked at the five elements and thought maybe the idea of training adjustment skills seemed a little difficult. Perhaps, if you're like most people, you may be tempted to train just one of the elements, maybe the easiest one?

The truth is, if you start by training just one, that will get the ball in motion. While most people would advise you to start with your beliefs, I think timing is the place to start. From the above graphs, you can see how important this is. I normally start here with the people I work with, and I have found that because it is so new, people respond well. One of the reasons is that it keeps us in the present rather than the past or the future. In addition, starting with timing is practical because you can measure it and improve it quickly. Small improvements and adjustments like this add up for everyone, not just for million dollar adjusters.

Since every small adjustment matters, ask yourself where you want to grow. How has this growth progressed? Is it moving forward, or has it stalled? What challenges are you facing that are preventing you from the growth you're seeking? To define that further, you may want to look at an "AS-IN" statement. These statements help us categorize the areas where growth is needed. For example, a professional baseball athlete might say, "In order to grow *as* a pitcher, I need to make adjustments *in* pitch accuracy." If you want to grow in the area of parenting, you could say, "In order to grow *as* a mom/dad, I need to make adjustments *in* selfless caregiving." Or, if your situation is more conditional, you could say, "In order to grow *as* a healthy person, I need to adjust *in* the area of weight loss."

Once you can define these growth goals as well as the areas that make them up, you will be closer to finding where your million dollar adjustment opportunity lies.

In the next chapter, you will learn that not all adjustments are created equal. You will see which ones have the greatest impact and how this can help you reach your million dollar adjustments more quickly. Knowing this can also help you show others how to reach theirs.

Ready? Let's go!

CHAPTER 8

Use Adjustments to Win. Period.

"Close doesn't count in baseball.
Close only counts in horseshoes and grenades."

—FRANK ROBINSON

"Do you mind if I demonstrate to you what an angry major-league manager looks like and yell in your face?" he asked me. I knew this was going to be interesting, but professional baseball was a constant exercise in adjustment for me. This was no different. Standing well over six feet tall and much stronger than me, the umpire supervisor was an intimidating force, and he was trained to be that way. He was trying to show me what younger umpires would face on the field and why they had to have their language skills down pat. "Sure," I casually replied. Then, I braced myself as he moved about a foot from my face. As he towered over me, he raised his voice and began to scream many things like, "You don't know what the *bleep* you're doing!

You're an idiot! That was a terrible call!" His breath hit my eyes and made me blink as droplets of spit hit my face. It went on for a few minutes, but I kept my eyes open and focused on his while listening to every word he said.

This is the real world for umpires. As the "third" team on the field, as I've heard them called, they compete with the other two teams for adherence to the rulebook, known as the Official Baseball Rules. Someone is always unhappy with them. So they have to know how to stay calm, hold their ground, and communicate the baseball rules. This takes practice, but it also takes a firm command of the language. That is why I was in that room that day. I needed to teach both the words and phrases and the emotional self-control that went with them. But I had to feel it first.

This type of language programming isn't typical. It requires customizing curriculums and adjusting to the needs of the learner. The example of an angry manager that I got that day was extremely important because it gave me the sense of context and urgency that was needed to allow young Latin umpires to be as prepared as possible to succeed. I wanted them to win, so I would have taken that screaming session a hundred times over to help them (but perhaps I would have suggested a breath mint!). From this and other interactions, I was able to adjust existing programs and customize them for umpires. With language barriers minimized or removed, they could get to the major leagues and secure great contracts. I love when adjustments create wins for people. I want adjustments to do the same for you.

Winning Through Growth

When you make adjustments, you can't help but grow. All growth usually involves modifications and even pivots at times. When you make adjustments, you can strengthen things like work skills, character, faith, confidence, joy, and the list goes on and on. When we have more of these things, we have a stronger starting position for our next adjustment, which can help us get to our goals a little faster, or at least a little easier. For example, after I learned what an angry manager looked, sounded, and felt like, the adjustments I was able to make helped young umpires grow, and I grew too. Growth in itself is a form of winning, and I don't know about you, but that makes it more attractive for me. It may not always be easy, but if after each little growth spurt (in whatever area you're growing), you are stronger than you were before and able to tackle the next thing with more confidence; it's worth it. Growth puts you on the path of winning because it has the power to influence your actions. Therefore, you should view your adjustments as a means to win.

I have found that how much we grow depends on the size and type of adjustment needed in any given situation. Remember that each of the five elements has a potency level that will increase or decrease depending on the size, duration, or type of adjustment needed. The great news is that you can estimate your wins better when you understand adjustment variations. Let's look at this a little closer.

Adjustment Size

The size of an adjustment is determined by its difficulty level. What makes an adjustment difficult for each person varies, but overall, it depends on how much effort, knowledge, and belief will be needed in order to accomplish it. The more that these are needed, the "bigger" the adjustment is.

I have found that when talking about adjustment, it is easier to classify the size of an adjustment into three simple categories: small, medium, and large. The actual size of the adjustment depends on the perception of the person making it, but overall, these three categories hold true. Logically, a small adjustment requires less than a large one. Here are my general guidelines when determining adjustment size:

Small Adjustments

A small adjustment means that minimal effort is needed. Strong belief isn't as necessary, great timing isn't as important, various strategies are not used, broad knowledge isn't needed, and lots of information may not need to be synthesized. An example of a small adjustment would be taking a well-marked detour when driving down the road.

Medium Adjustments

A medium adjustment requires more than a small adjustment. This includes slightly more belief and timing, an increase in current knowledge, possible alteration of strategy, and stronger information synthesis than the small adjustment. Using the driving example, a medium adjustment would be stumbling upon a road closing without a marked detour and having to find an alternative route. Here, the driver needs to know alternative routes, possibly continue with or change to an offensive strategy, and believe that the alternative route will be successful.

Large Adjustments

A large adjustment stretches the elements, creating a high potency level. Strong belief is needed, more knowledge and information synthesis is required, a strategy change is likely, and great timing is necessary. Continuing with the driving example, encountering an accident that just happened or being involved in the accident would require a large adjustment. Here, the driver may need to get out of the car, check on passengers, know to call the police and give a report, maybe move debris out of the road, as well as believe in himself/herself or others to signal oncoming traffic to go around the accident or to wait.

These simple classifications are important when talking about adjustment because they give us an idea of the growth that can happen. If you are making a small adjustment, there may be some growth because you may see or do something you haven't done before, as in the detour example above. But generally, it isn't going to create deep learning or growth unless you do it over and over again. It is shallow, especially if it occurs just once or twice. By contrast, a large adjustment may be more uncomfortable than a small adjustment because it requires more of you. Being in a car accident or helping with one is more emotional, more physical, more mental, and maybe even more spiritual, thereby creating deeper growth and learning. This means that you will have the ability to recall it and apply newly gained experiential learning more so than a smaller adjustment.

Adjustment Duration

Going through an adjustment takes varying amounts of time. Some people go through them quickly, while others make them more slowly. This is where our internal clocks come into play. We generally make adjustments according to comfortable, natural rhythms, and we will default to that unless we are pushed to make them faster or slower. Once you know that there are five elements of adjustment, you can begin to see why duration makes sense. There's more going on than meets the eye!

Like the simple classification of adjustment size, I have also chosen to classify adjustment duration in three simple categories for ease of use: quick, punctual, and slow.

Quick Adjustments

A quick adjustment means that the five elements are utilized and implemented in a short time frame. Generally, a quick adjustment occurs anywhere between a few seconds to a few days.

Punctual Adjustments

A punctual adjustment is slightly longer than a quick one, lasting anywhere between a week and a few months. Either one or all five elements may need a little more time to move through the adjustment.

Slow Adjustments

These adjustments generally take around three months to a year. This is caused by a lag in one or more of the five elements due to a variety of reasons.

Over time, as adjustment skills are honed, the duration may decrease, especially if it is similar to a past adjustment. This makes sense because of the knowledge element. It is also important to note that overall health and well-being can affect adjustment duration. Big life changes or anything that disrupts our internal chemistry might alter our normal ability to adjust for a time. More on this in the next chapter.

Adjustment Type

To reach our goals, we need to make one of two types of adjustments. We either need to make a one-time adjustment or a repeated, modified adjustment.

One-Time Adjustment

A one-time adjustment is generally one that you haven't done before and that only needs to happen once to be effective. The five elements come together to accomplish something specific. For example, assembling a piece of furniture in a few easy steps (don't you love those instructions that come in the box?!). One-time adjustments are less common than repeated, modified adjustments.

Repeated, Modified Adjustment

This type of adjustment occurs when we need to make a series of adjustments in order to accomplish our goals. It includes those adjustments that we just made but with a slight modification. The five elements of adjustment are constantly being challenged until a goal is reached. Examples of these types of adjustments are learning how to dance, swing a baseball bat, or communicate effectively.

Winning Through Mastery

Now that we know how adjustments can vary, we can use this information to help us understand the impact adjustments can have in any situation. These help you to understand the art of adjusting. When we master the art of adjusting, we can shorten the duration of any adjustment, big or small. The Element Impact

Matrix that was developed for transformative teaching utilized the three categories of size, duration, and type.

We often think of mastery just in terms of a skill or profession, like a golfer or a doctor. Through training, a person becomes a "master." We think of masters as people who sit at the highest level of their profession and are the beacon of success or wisdom. In other words, they are the masters of their craft. We could call the million dollar adjusters the masters of their sport.

Masters have not only succeeded in their specific area of expertise, but they have mastered the art of adjustment without realizing it. Every master has had to make millions of adjustments in order to become the skilled guru of today. On the path to mastery, we all meet change, uncertainty, and failure, and through adjusting well to these things, we find a way to keep going and win. The beauty of great adjustments is that they can lead to mastery, depending on the depth of the adjustment.

Adjustment Depth

To master something, great adjustments that are made must stay in your long-term memory so that you can recall them when needed. In other words, they have to go deep. Adjustments that get to our long-term memory are the ones that we recall often or have some other properties associated with them—like emotions or even scents!

In addition to having deeply encoded great adjustments in our memories, we need our poorer adjustments stay a little shallow. This means that while they are important learning events, we need not attach significant relevance to them in a way that stops us from moving forward.

You may have heard the phrase, "Step out of your comfort zone," when it comes to trying new things in order to grow or reach a goal. That phrase just means that you are letting in risk so that you can learn how to adjust to it. If you know how to make good adjustments, risk is minimized because you have the skills and confidence to ride through the ups and downs. The road to mastery is easier! Those people who have the adjustment skill set can apply it when needed. These people live their calling and seem to do it effortlessly.

To become a master at something, you must initially embrace adjustments of all sizes, in all durations and all types. In the process, you will find the ones that work well for you. Flush out the ones that don't produce fruit in your life and reinforce the ones that do.

Winning by Lifting Others Up

If you've ever watched someone as they are going through an adjustment, their pattern and adjustment skill level may frustrate you—especially if it is different from yours. You may have timing or outcome expectations that they don't. Or they may make adjustments so much easier than you do. This makes sense since we all have different adjustment patterns. Perhaps this is why Dave Hansen told me that life is about patience as well as adjustments. We need patience when making our adjustments and watching others make theirs. We can't just focus on the "me" part of the word adjustMEnt; we have to focus on the "US" as well.

Helping Others

There are many ways you can help others in their adjustment process. The first is simply to share the word adjustment, and talk about its meaning and application in their lives. The second is to tell them about the five elements and suggest they learn about their own pattern. Finally, sharing what you learned about training and growing each element will be very helpful to them as they work on their own adjustment muscles.

We all win when we share our own stories and examples of growth and mastery. If we are working with a team, a family, or any group of people for a common purpose, we have the opportunity to employ adjustment concepts. By doing so, there is a common language, and all efforts are better understood, creating more harmony and peace in the long run. We can help each other see where elements need a little more strength and help each other get there. That is a big win!

Interestingly enough, in my work with adjustment, I have found a few nuances when sharing the word "adjustment" and its corresponding meaning with different demographics. Let me explain.

Gender

I found that sharing the word "adjustment" with men initiated a different response than sharing the same word with women. Men seemed to have an instant understanding or at least an acceptance of the word. Sharing the word "adjustment" with women didn't produce the same response. I found that words that resonated better were "pivot" or modification. I'm not sure why that is but this disconnect was interesting and caused me to reword how I approached the subject with women. As a woman myself, I didn't really feel a sense of connection to the word at first. If you remember back in chapter 1, I talked about how I had no particular reaction to the word adjustment at first either.

As I researched why this is, I found two possible reasons why this word didn't connect. The first reason is that our mothers didn't use this word much in their vocabularies other than when it came to fashion (for example, "adjust your skirt"). Teachers didn't use this word much either, other than in science or math ("adjust your calculation"). Simply put, it is unfamiliar to us in a positive and empowering way, rather than a negative or neutral way.

The other reason that women didn't have an instant response to this word is that understanding its benefit doesn't come easily. Words like "love" and "work" have instant outcomes attached. Therefore, we can connect with them. Adjustment doesn't bring to mind specific outcomes for women. However, I found that when I talked about the pattern types like Steady Eddy or Maverick, this seemed to be the key to opening the conversation and connection to the word adjustment. Women, like men, want to know themselves better and are used to hearing about relational tests like the Enneagram or DISC. By using the pattern type names, I was able to bridge the gap while being careful not to "box someone in." Pattern types are generalizations and are not meant to serve as labels, but they do help to get great conversations started.

As women, we communicate differently than men. Today, we are being challenged in new ways and the word adjustment may now make more sense than ever. With the ever-increasing amount of analytics measuring everything we all do, we will be making adjustments in our lives that we never prepared for, so this is a great time to begin the conversation with everyone.

Global Adjustments

I think I'm especially aware of global culture because of the international work I've done over the years. Culture is tied to language, and this is why some words resonate and some don't. People of other races and cultures have words that resonate with them, while other words don't. For example, some American coaches would say the words, "Grind through it," which resonate with English-speaking, American-born players. But the phrase lost its impact on the Latin players because it didn't carry the same meaning. The word "grind" didn't translate with the same power. Trust me, I know because I tried demonstrating it in every creative way I could think of!

When talking about adjustments with people from other races and cultures, sometimes we have to set the stage and help the word have the impact it should. This is why I encourage the practice of simply talking about adjustment and its meaning. Showing how it applies to any situation can help someone begin to see its importance. Common vocabulary inside of a language is very important because we make associations based on the use of words. For example, if you were born and raised in America, you know that the word "hot" has a few meanings. The same goes for the word "sick." We associate people and situations with both the literal and slang meaning of words.

On occasion I have been asked, "Should I learn about other adjustment patterns so that I can understand and work better with everyone?" This is a difficult question to answer because it is a common practice to think that if we know other people's patterns, then we will be more sympathetic and understanding regarding their differences. Indeed, if this is our purpose, then, by all means, the answer is yes. But we should understand that your adjustment pattern already factors in how well you will adjust to new situations and people, so you should be careful not to change your behavior to suit everyone else's patterns around you. You could simply hone your own. However, if your goal is to work with a certain individual more effectively, it may help to understand where your adjustment pattern might be different from theirs, but more so in what specific elements. For example, if you have a strong belief element and they do not, you can talk about this element and share how it impacts your actions. The same is true conversely if they have a stronger belief element than you. This is powerful when working with others.

Winning Through Endurance

Baseball is a long season. Games start in April and end in late October. In addition, there is training before the season and after it. Performing at a high level throughout the season requires both physical and mental endurance. In fact, in 2016, *Sports Illustrated* published an article regarding new research that showed that a tired brain can hinder performance as much as a tired muscle.[11]

The same is true in anything that we must focus on for a time. Whether it is a new business, building a great relationship, getting in shape, or doing a great job at work, having successful outcomes requires endurance.

---

[11] Ian McMahan, "Figuring Out Fatigue: A Tired Brain Can Hinder Performance as much as a Tired Muscle," *Sports Illustrated*, September 27, 2016, https://www.si.com/edge/2016/09/27/mental-fatigue-sports-tired-athlete-brain-training-warriors-leicester-city.

Endurance is the ability to tolerate or go through something challenging. In some languages, it is similar to the word, suffer. To suffer is to endure. The truth is, none of us wants to suffer. But it is what develops the other areas of ourselves that we need in order to make great adjustments. For example, belief and possibly timing. When we endure a hard season of life, we learn that we are capable, which creates confidence. This confidence feeds our belief system and fans the flame of hope when we face new challenges. In other words, endurance is a way to win. When we have confidence and hope, we are more willing to continue making adjustments, moving us closer to mastery.

There are times when our beliefs can go dim, and through the Signature PAR test, we are able to see approximately where that happens in an individual. If you go back to the graphics from the last chapter, you may remember seeing it in the early draft pick's timing results. By knowing when and where belief unravels, we can help others see it and create a way around it. More on this in the next chapter.

Through growth, mastery, lifting others up, and endurance, we see that winning by adjustment isn't just for high performers. It is for everyone. When you understand the types of adjustment and their respective elements, you are equipped in ways you've never been before.

CHAPTER 9

Finding Joy in Big Seasons of Adjustment

"Life is either a daring adventure or nothing at all."

—HELEN KELLER

Looking out the van window, I could see the sunbeams dancing on the beautiful waters that touched the shores of the Dominican Republic. Driving along Highway 3, known in the Dominican Republic as La Autopista Las Américas, was always a scenic treat, especially along the shoreline. The palm trees swayed gently as the coconut vendors pushed their carts along, looking for thirsty customers to tempt with their tropical drink. Fish sellers had the catch of the day hanging from strings on display and ready for purchase. The streets were always active, and my driver had upbeat bachata music playing loudly as cars and motorcycles swerved in and out of lanes, honking horns to tell others to move out of the way.

After nearly an hour's drive, I arrived at the baseball academy. The players were in uniform on the field, and the local staff welcomed me as I entered the administrative buildings. I went into the classrooms to set up materials for teachers that would be arriving later that day.

While working in the classroom, Yeison, a player who wasn't practicing that day due to a leg injury, came by to say hello. He had played last season in the United States, and after a quick greeting, we started talking about his first season stateside. I asked him to tell me about his greatest challenge. In Spanish, he told me that he missed his native foods, his music, family, and friends. He said that even though he had heard many times that playing in the United States was going to be a big adjustment, and he thought he was prepared, he realized he wasn't. There were some situations that he encountered, and he didn't know what to do. When I asked Yeison what he would have done differently, he said he would have asked for more help before he left the island and while he was here in the US.

Yeison's story is not an uncommon one. I have heard similar comments from players whose team helps prepare them through language, culture, and life programs, but once the actual change comes, they find themselves having a hard time adjusting to the new environment. Why is this?

We Can't Prepare for Everything

Programs that prepare people for big, new seasons of growth are certainly helpful, but the reality is, they can't anticipate everything that might occur. And ultimately, there will be situations that weren't included in the program. This is the same for parenting and so many other areas of life as well. We can prepare only so much with foundational knowledge and training, but then we have to be ready to make adjustments when surprise situations occur.

As a teacher of culture, I taught players about the culture shock curve, which explained the phases one might go through when experiencing daily adjustments. Foreign living can be a shock to the emotional, physical, psychological, and spiritual aspects of a person's being as they try to find some normalcy. One of the things we always suggested was to find some joy in every day as a way to ease the process. Simple joys could be the laughter of a friend, dancing to a favorite song on high volume, or the beauty of a landscape. I think that of all people I've met, baseball people know how to find joy in the grind of a season. I was always laughing with them. Humor is a good thing for all of us.

Over the years, I had players who faced big seasons of adjustment. Whether through loss (like losing a parent or sibling), sudden success (like moving up a few levels), or other life changes (health issues, getting married, having a baby, and so on), I have seen that with big seasons of adjustment—especially ones that involve loss—our internal timing can get off track. In fact, loss ranks at the top of the list when it comes to internal timing change.

The first time I had a player experience a big loss was in my second year of teaching. A Venezuelan player's father suddenly had a heart attack. He was very close to his father, and this was devastating to him. His shock and grief changed his demeanor for a time, and the baseball organization gave him a few weeks off from playing, which helped some, but ultimately his whole season wasn't the same. This makes sense since grief is a very strong and powerful emotion—especially when it comes as a shock. Knowing that support is vital during grief, I tried to stay in contact more often with this player and encouraged him to write about his emotions and feelings so that he could process them. I purchased a journal for him to do this and talked to him about what to do. But still, his motivation evaporated, and he had no energy to make adjustments. As we know, adjustments require internal timing, and in grief, it can all but stop.

In 2020, my daughter, Jordan, and her husband, Matt, worked through intense grief when they lost two pregnancies back to back. One happened in early January, and the other happened in June. Normally a very active person, Jordan was listless. Her internal timing seemed like it stopped. Her heart was broken, and her body had been through a lot. It almost stopped me as well. Our entire family was hurting for her and her husband and dealing with our own sadness. It was hard to help because nothing made her feel better, and my own timing was gut-punched. I knew that it would take time for her and all of us, but especially her. She was devastated, and I learned that pregnancy loss should never be taken lightly by family or friends.

I thought back to the many times I worked with players who were grieving and the pressure they faced during these times, and I tried to pull up something that might be helpful to her. I knew that jump-starting internal timing in stages of grief isn't realistic, so I just told her to try to do one normal thing every day. This would give her a focal point, which would cause her to use some energy on timing. It seemed to resonate with her. She felt she could do one normal thing per day. This gave her a doable strategy to help her deal with her grief, which she needed. Jordan started with one normal thing a day, and within a week, she was doing a few normal things each day. Her internal timing was slowly picking up as she maintained focus and activity.

Initially, Jordan felt as though she had failed and didn't know what to do to improve her odds in the future. Her belief took a big hit. But as she started to focus on and learn more about the causes of pregnancy loss (knowledge), she sifted through information (information synthesis) and started working with a few doctors to create a plan (strategic actions). Somewhere between three and four months after the initial trauma, she was able to find some joy. Finally, almost nine months later, her belief returned. She was making adjustments all along, but when the final element (belief) became stronger due to the success in the other things she was doing, her heart and soul began to heal.

Joy On Deck

The truth is that nobody likes to change or make adjustments. I have learned that most people would love to succeed right out of the gate on their first try. I put myself in the same group. Easy wins reduce the possibility of anxiety, right?

With so many disruptors today, we are looking for normalcy and calm, let alone joy. However, if we don't find joy in our lives on a regular basis, this will impact our motivation, and we will not be able to make great adjustments. Seeing so many others struggle with adversity, I have been reminded of the power of joy over and over again. After going through such a tough season of loss, I found myself reflecting on it and asking questions. What is this power, and how do you regain it in big seasons of adjustment? How does it emerge through trials?

I believe there are two types of joy: conditional and non-conditional. Conditional joy depends on a situation that occurs—like the laughter of a child, a puppy playing, or a beautiful sunset. These are conditional and depend on an event (or a condition) to occur in order to experience joy. Conditional joy is important because it allows us to laugh, let off some steam, and feel good for a time. It helps to rejuvenate us and provides a break from the stresses of life. We can feel this type of joy by doing nothing or after accomplishing anything, including an adjustment that went well.

Non-conditional joy is a deeper joy. It is ongoing contentment that doesn't require an event to occur in order for it to be present. This type of joy is a state of being that doesn't extinguish as easily through most smaller adjustments. It comes from deep within our inner self, formed by our beliefs, past experiences, and unshakeable peace. We experience this joy from focusing on it through faith and actions of faith as well as surviving difficult things in the past.

When we experience situations where we have to make big adjustments, deep joy can be thrown off, especially if these adjustments challenge our core beliefs. When deep joy is thrown off, sometimes simple, conditional joy is what starts to bring us back around.

My daughter had a deep faith and deep joy before the back-to-back losses she experienced. These losses made her question her beliefs about life, death, and God's goodness. In other words, they shook her belief system. She had to find a way to realign her past beliefs with her present condition. While the deep joy was in a state of realignment, the smaller, conditional joys came back into her life first. This is usually the case. Through hugs, visits with friends and family, songs, small getaways, and laughter, these smaller, conditional joys softened the blow on a daily basis. Finally, her deep joy returned. But it didn't look the same as it did before. It was less frivolous but more rooted. Deep roots make great trees, don't they?

Since adjustments are a part of life, then joy must be part of the equation. Why is that? Because joy helps reset our timing when our beliefs are wonky. Joy is a gift. It emerges when we start seeing it in small ways and then rewire our hearts in big ways from there. To notice these small joys, we have to do three simple things:

Take time to be in the present

Many people might call this mindfulness, but it could also be a result of adventure or time in faith. When your thoughts are turned to the "off" position, and your attention is fixed on something external (like the puppies playing together or that incredible sunset), you are being present. Your attention could also be internal (concentrating on your breathing, heartbeat, or the feeling of an emotion), which is also another way of being present. Thoughts that are turned "off" leave you free from to-do lists, worries, or self-talk and open to the world around you or the life inside of you.

Think about joy, even if you don't feel it yet

It has been said that what we think about is what we attract. If you are thinking about life's joys, you will likely notice them and allow them to occur in your life. For example, a songbird in the morning can be a joy or a disturbance, depending on how you think about it. To experience joy through adjustments, you have to think about it, even if you don't feel it all the time. That might mean laughing, even if you are just mildly amused. In doing so, you train your brain to recognize and respond to joy.

When you do feel joy, feel it down to the heart level whenever possible

It's hard to feel joy when we have heavy burdens weighing down our hearts. In order to truly feel joy, we have to unburden ourselves. Heavy loads do not allow for light-heartedness, which is what joy gives us. When you are in a moment of joy, the best thing you can do is feel it in your heart, down to your core. If something is funny, laugh until your ribs hurt. If something is inspiring, allow yourself to be awed. If you love someone, allow yourself to feel that love deeply. Joy like this is healing.

Have you ever had a challenging experience that shook your beliefs? Maybe you didn't get that job you really wanted, and that made you question your abilities. What did that experience do to your energy? Did your energy levels plummet or flatline? Or perhaps you experienced the opposite: for some, difficult experiences result in increased energy, depending on their beliefs. Maybe you align more with this.

Either way, beliefs very much influence our internal timing. Beliefs either drive us or create roadblocks. When our beliefs are in a state of limbo or have just gone through some shaking, we can feel it in our timing. The sooner we can tap into our timing, the sooner we can get back on track. There are various ways to do that, but when coupled with some form of joy, they are more effective. Joy is like the pressure valve of life. It is the great connector from a red light to a green light.

Contagious Joy

One thing that became clear to me when I first started administering the Signature PAR test was that results that didn't seem quite right had some similarities. These odd test results usually meant the test taker had something else deeper going on in his/her life. It made sense. After noticing this and running data, we saw too many outliers in these situations. So we changed our protocols and would not allow anyone experiencing illness, trauma, or a big life change to take a baseline test. The results would not be accurate nor fair. We would not be serving others well if we didn't take this into account. The international players, in particular, were acutely aware of this.

Most of the international players that I worked with were going through big seasons of adjustment. Far from home, missing family, and enduring the first long season with very few days off would wear on them by July. The earlier joking and banter with each other that initially helped them laugh and let off steam now made them mad. Weariness has a way of making things look different.

Big seasons of adjustment that go on for a time create a weariness that may not allow you to see the conditional joy, no matter how hard you look. When this happened with the Latin players, in particular, I noticed two things that they did that helped them. First, they served each other somehow, whether it was on the field or off the field. This service was in the form of haircuts, cooking for each other, or driving each other to errands (not all international players had a driver's license). Second, they had music. Playful in spirit, they would put on music and dance, sing, or gently "play the drums" by banging their hands on the table. Yes, this was a form of rhythm, which makes sense why it impacted timing. However, it created conditional joy for them. When one person started smiling and dancing, the next person started to loosen up, and before long, the group was in on it. This is what I call *contagious joy*.

Joy that doesn't spontaneously originate from within can sometimes be ignited by seeing it in others. Since we all operate with some form of "herd mentality," that can work with joy as well. Think about it: Has there ever been a time where you saw someone laughing, and it made you laugh? Or someone who grabbed you while you were in a bad mood and made you start dancing? Then you were the receiver of contagious joy. Whether we are the giver or the receiver of contagious joy, it helps give the weary in spirit a little refreshing. This is an important part of moving through a tough and long adjustment period.

Nicholas Christakis, a professor at Harvard Medical School, coauthored a happiness study that backs up this idea of contagious joy. He found that "everyday interactions we have with other people are definitely contagious, in terms of happiness." Researchers at Harvard University and the University of California, San Diego, document how happiness spreads through social networks and had metrics to back it up. They found that when a person becomes happy, a friend living close by has a 25 percent higher chance of becoming happy themselves! A spouse experiences an 8 percent increased chance, and for next-door neighbors, it's 34 percent.[12] We should remember that we can serve others who are going through big adjustments with simple, contagious joy.

In order to spread contagious joy, we must first be infected by it. That means you have to be around joyful people and allow that joy to penetrate your soul. Not sure where to go to get infected? Look for people in love, people with great purpose, people who build others up, or people who serve others with great faith. These people are already infected with joy, and by being near them, you can "catch it."

---

[12] James H. Fowler and Nicholas A. Christakis, "Dynamic Spread of Happiness in a Large Social Network: Longitudinal Analysis Over 20 Years in the Framingham Heart Study," *British Medical Journal* 337, no. a2338 (December 5, 2008). https://doi.org/10.1136/bmj.a2338.

Joyful Adjustment Patterns

In the years of documenting adjustment pattern tendencies, joyful tendencies surfaced. While every pattern experiences joy, the All-Star and Steady Eddy pattern types seem to experience slightly deeper joy while the other pattern types tend to experience conditional joy more often. Of course, this isn't the case 100 percent of the time, but it is an interesting generalization.

The good news is that all adjustment types can give and receive contagious joy. Joy keeps us from becoming overwhelmed or anxious. When we have joy in our lives, making adjustments through loss or weariness comes a little easier. Joy helps us move forward.

However, there are times in life when, depending on the type of adjustments that have to be made, it is not wise to move forward as before. This can happen when adjustment efforts that have been made consistently yield little success or when the necessary adjustments go against someone's belief systems. In fact, there are five possible scenarios in which drawing the line on adjustments, if at least for a time, might be the healthiest option. This is the case when someone chooses to draw the line on adjustments and walk away to pursue another avenue altogether. I've seen players voluntarily decide to leave the game after years of trying to get into the major leagues. No matter what adjustments they made, they couldn't reach the level of play needed, and they decided to pursue another road. In doing so, they drew the line on adjustments.

If you've ever had a time when you were feeling inner conflict with certain adjustments, then turn the page. You will find some answers on when to draw the line on adjustments in your own life.

CHAPTER 10

Drawing the Line
on Adjustments

"You can do anything, but not everything."

—UNKNOWN

Sitting on a plane from Austin, Texas, to Chicago, I met an executive from a large tech company. We were about the same age, and we struck up a casual conversation about kids and parenting today. The topic of culture came into the forefront, and we both reflected on the massive cultural shifts in progress and how our kids would be navigating those. The conversation went one step further as we shared how *we* were navigating these changes.

Steve was a senior director of global sales, and you can bet he's met people from all over the world. He worked with people from different cultures, ages, and races, and it seemed to me that he was pretty adaptable. But as our conversation continued, he shared that his company paired him up with a change counselor to help him move through all the new shifts. I was a little surprised by this. I asked him, "What changes are you having the most difficulty with?" He looked away for a minute and said, "Honestly, I think it's the gender pronoun changes. For example, we all have to wear name tags with our preferred pronouns, and in meetings, I have to use these pronouns as we talk to each other. It's so hard to do that throughout the entire meeting. It's never something I had to think about before, and it doesn't come easy. So, of course, I slip up and use the wrong pronoun sometimes. I just don't think it's necessary to make everyone else change their normal vocabulary for the few people who are concerned about it, you know?"

There it was. Steve had drawn the line on his willingness to make adjustments, even if he didn't think so. It was 2019, and he had achieved success in his career for decades, and I'm sure he had seen and adapted to all kinds of change. Most of these adjustments were gradual and not against his deeply held ideals. Sudden and challenging changes in the workplace were causing his adjustment abilities to buckle. I'm sure he wasn't alone if the company provided him with a change counselor. Forced change was testing him. And this was *before* the 2020 pandemic!

The Force of Five

Change management is not a new concept in organizations. In fact, it's been around since the 1990s, when the human side of change moved out of academia and into business. From big companies like General Electric to individual authors and consultants, the language and topics of change grew popular in this decade.

Then in the 2000s, change management became a formalized discipline.[13] Resources were provided to create structure, tools, projects, and practitioners within organizations. Change management became a profession, and related associations, standards, and certifications emerged to establish this as an important department inside of a business. The goal of this department was to help people make change more effectively in order to increase productivity and profit while reducing risk. People are the backbone of a business, and without their participation in change, new programs or investments can fail. In a data-driven world, business owners and shareholders are looking at numbers to evaluate many aspects of the company and its people. From the data, they decide the direction of the company, operations, and investments.

The question is, what if people like the way things are—like my plane friend Steve? They may be willing to make some adjustments to be a team player or keep their job, but what about those adjustments they may *not* be willing to make? Will they lose opportunities or even their job? You can bet that many people have asked that question over the years. There is a silent cap on change for everyone, no matter how perfectly it might be pitched.

Through the Signature PAR test, I've noticed five situations where people stumble with change and stop making adjustments. Interestingly, they all start with the letter "F"! As you will discover, adjustment is not the same as change, but they are close cousins. The five adjustment-stopping conditions are: faith/belief, fatigue, faculties, fear, and the familiar. They have a

---

[13] "The History and Future of Change Management," Prosci. https://www.prosci.com/resources/articles/change-management-history-and-future.

force strong enough to hold off on adjustment. Let's take a closer look at each one.

Faith

In the United States, we have the freedom to practice religion and faith in whatever manner we choose. This is an enormous benefit of being American. Because of this gift, we can abstain from things that are in direct contradiction to our beliefs. Our spirituality is part of what makes us human, and it is very important to our well-being, so I believe we must care for it like any other aspect of our lives.

This means that if we are asked to adjust to something that isn't in line with our faith-based beliefs, we may have to draw the line on it and find a different compromise. Have you ever had a time where you were asked to do something that went against your faith or strongly held beliefs? If so, something in you probably felt uncomfortable.

This happened to me in one of the first jobs I had. I was asked to report a falsehood about something that happened in the workplace. As a Christian, this went against my faith, and I had to say no to that. This was a request I could not honor, and the only adjustment was to communicate that. Could I have faced repercussions? Yes, I could have. I could have lost my job and coworkers whom I liked working with. However, my beliefs are my compass in life, and if I allowed them to be compromised, I would lose my integrity, which is why certain adjustments should not be made. Luckily, I did not lose my job, and I was never asked to lie again.

Recently, Piers Morgan, an English broadcaster, journalist, and television figure, walked away from his job while on camera. It happened when talking about an interview between a member of the royal family and a well-known television personality. He did not believe statements that were made about the British royal family and felt that these statements were in direct conflict with what he knew and felt about his country and its monarchy. His employer asked him to apologize, but he couldn't make this adjustment and do that. He very publicly drew the line on adjustments and quit his job. His beliefs did not allow him to apologize for something he felt was incorrect.

Our faith and values affect us because they are part of our identity. They impact how we live our lives and how we behave. It is important to understand the connection between faith and adjustments because life will test them often. If an adjustment doesn't "feel" right, it may be because it goes against a strong belief that you hold. I've always told my kids that they should never make an adjustment that requires them to compromise their faith. Take some time to know where you stand in your faith and beliefs so that you are prepared when situations like this occur.

Now it's your turn. What is one area of your faith or belief that would stop you from making an adjustment? Take a minute to think about this. Then write it on the lines below. Knowing our limits before they are challenged is important so that we can be prepared.

_____

_____

_____

_____

_____

_____

Fatigue

It's not difficult to imagine that being tired would affect some-one's ability to make adjustments. When we are tired, we aren't mentally prepared for the effort that adjustment requires. In the last chapter, we talked about weariness and how joy can help us get our timing back on track. While joy can certainly help get us through times of weariness, we may not make the best adjust-ments in those times. Sometimes we need to push through, and sometimes we just can't.

In fact, in 2016, *Sports Illustrated* published research showing that a tired brain can hinder performance as much as a tired muscle.[14] If you've ever had a tired brain, you can relate. This article talked about research done by Dr. Andrew Coutts, who reported his work in the *Journal of Sports Sciences*. He found that since the brain collects physical sensations of the body and decides how much is too much, cognitive fatigue can impair an athlete's ability to react well and be in top physical states. Dr. Samuele Marcora, another researcher on the project, said that "physiologically you may be fine but mentally fatigued athletes find the same task much more effortful."

Mental fatigue impacts our ability to make great adjustments. Dr. Marcora suggests that mental fatigue can develop from sleep deprivation, video games, and having to perform an unfamiliar or difficult activity. In addition, any mentally demanding sport can induce mental fatigue.

Do you find that you have less desire to be "at your best" when you are tired? You may want to be, but without rest, it isn't possible. If you have had a hard time making adjustments, it may

---

[14] McMahan, "Figuring Out Fatigue."

be due to mental fatigue. You may draw the line on adjustments when you're tired.

Many of the international athletes that I work with experience underlying mental fatigue from living in another country, especially in their first season. Together with mastering a new language and culture and playing with people at a higher performance level, this creates additional mental fatigue and impacts their overall success.

From the testing we have done, it is interesting to note that fatigue can be seen in the way people take the test. When people are tired, they have less patience for new tasks that don't always seem relevant to them at the moment. This is one reason we don't test those who are under strain or unusual circumstances. Drawing the line on adjustments is attractive for those who are mentally fatigued. If you are or have been tired, take some time to rest. Look at the five elements of adjustment and see which ones will take the most effort for you to improve upon and do those last. As you see improvements in the other areas, you will have more energy to tackle the harder ones.

How much do you have going on in your life right now? Can you handle more adjustments? What is one thing you could let go of to get more rest? Take some time to think this through and jot it down here:

_____

_____

_____

_____

_____

_____

Faculties

Have you ever felt like you wanted to do something but didn't think you had enough talent or ability? Maybe your skills weren't as sharp as they needed to be? If so, how did you feel about making adjustments to get better? For example, if you wanted to be a great singer but couldn't hit a range of notes, would you keep trying?

Often, people will draw the line on adjustment if they feel they can't master a skill or increase their talent enough to be successful. The Signature PAR test has shown us this time and time again. We make perceptions about our abilities and the journey we think it will require to improve them, and then we judge the amount and type of adjustments it will take to get there. If we feel it requires too much effort, we may draw the line on adjustments. Sometimes this makes sense, and we should focus on the areas of our lives where our gifts and talents can flourish. However, if we know that we do have talent in an area, that it is our gift, we should be pursuing higher levels of talent. How do we do that? Have you ever wondered about that?

In 2006, a psychology professor named Carol Dweck wrote a book called Mindset: The New Psychology of Success. In this book, she talks about fixed mindset and growth mindset. The difference is that a fixed mindset believes that individual abilities are static and can't change. For people with this belief system, success is just the affirmation of that set of abilities and talent. A growth mindset, on the other hand, believes that individual talents and abilities can be stretched and grown into success. It doesn't see failure as a reflection of a lack of skills or talent but as a springboard for growth. In addition, organizations that practice a growth mindset will develop the abilities of the people inside of it, rather than simply relying only on the natural talent that is hired in. Hence, another reason for change management personnel inside of an organization. A growth mindset can encourage people to want to continue to learn and become life-long learners.

If you feel you can't master a skill due to a lack of ability or because the bar keeps changing, then you may decide to draw the line on adjustments. Sometimes you may be right. Other times, perhaps a growth mindset would be helpful to see the possibilities.

What skill or talent do you feel you are gifted with and what skill/talent would you like to improve? Feel free to make a few notes as you reflect on this.

_____

_____

_____

_____

_____

_____

Fear

I've often had people ask me if adjustment is the same as change. The answer is yes and no. Yes, because adjustments can lead to change. No, because change doesn't always involve adjustments. For example, if your belt is too loose, you can adjust it to fit and keep wearing it. Or you could go into your closet and change your belt altogether. Adjustments help us work with what we have to either create something new or lead us to change.

This distinction is important because many people fear change. The fear of change is called metathesiophobia and is classified as a disorder. That doesn't mean that if you are uncomfortable with change, you automatically have this condition. I only mention it here because, for those with this condition, it is important to understand that adjustment is not the same as change.

In fact, our predispositions teach us to resist change in order to feel in control. But the normal fear of change becomes full-blown when it is irrational, persistent, and very intense. People who fear change of any kind will most likely draw the line on adjustments. In addition, people who may not normally fear change may fear making certain adjustments if the potential outcome creates anxiety for them. Perhaps you've had an experience where you were asked to make an adjustment, but you didn't know how the outcome would impact you. Maybe in school, you had an opportunity to take a higher-level class but didn't want others to think you were "too" smart? Or maybe if you've always wanted to lose weight but fear the attention you might receive as a result? Perhaps you want to retire but fear not having a clear daily purpose? Fear can be powerful, especially if we can't see the outcomes clearly.

Fear of the unknown is common. If you are fearful of what might happen if you don't make a mandated adjustment, like job or friend loss, take some time to reflect on this. It could be that these mandated adjustments go against your beliefs, or perhaps something else is at play. If the adjustment will negatively impact your life, perhaps you are right in drawing the line on it.

If fear, however, has influenced you to draw the line on a healthy adjustment, try making small adjustments first. This could be as simple as writing down how you will attack the next adjustment before it happens. Fear causes us to live in defensive strategies, and in doing so, we might miss an opportunity to grow.

Another way to combat fear when making a healthy adjustment is to adopt some positive statements. Here are a few examples that others have used:

> *I allow myself permission to fail sometimes as I adjust*
> *and improve.*
> *I will prepare for growth over outcome.*
> *I created the pressure. I can remove it.*
> *I respect myself for trying new things.*

Are any fears stopping you from making a *healthy* adjustment? What strategies have you been using to combat fear? Again, feel free to jot down your thoughts.

_____

_____

_____

_____

_____

_____

Familiar

As a learning consultant, I strive to make sure that all learning is transferable. What does this mean? It means that what is learned inside a classroom or computer does not stop there; it is transferred to the real world. In essence, it's applying our learning to new situations. This is the point of learning, isn't it? The idea of using familiar information to solve problems, help people, reduce risk, or create new things is the true value of education to the world.

However, familiar information can also cause us to make judgments on situations before we have a chance to adjust to them. For example, if a young child is bitten by a neighbor's dog, s/he may learn that dogs can be dangerous and might be apprehensive around all dogs. The child takes the learning from a past experience and applies it to similar new situations. Therefore, for that child, it may be hard to adjust to new dogs. Another situation might be work-related. A salesperson, for example, might find that the more sales s/he makes, the more s/he has to travel. Unwilling to leave home as much may cause someone to simply draw the line on bigger sales and, therefore, on making the adjustments that are needed in order to do that.

Is there something in your past learning that makes you leery of situations where you could face it again? Do you avoid opportunities to grow or advance due to these experiences?

Many adjustments draw on a person's past learning (element: knowledge). If a prior outcome was negative, that learning may cause him/her to draw the line on similar situations. Maybe you know this firsthand. If that happens, that means you may be unwilling to make an adjustment in a similar situation. This is an example of the power of transferable learning. Transferable learning has important implications for teaching. One such implication is allowing enough time for someone to process information in a way that doesn't rush them. They may need extra time for the complex cognitive activity of information integration.

Information integration theory was developed and tested by Norman Anderson. This theory states that when we obtain new information, those new pieces of information will affect our attitudes. It also tells us that each bit of information has two important qualities, weight and value. Both factors influence our attitudes.

It's interesting to note that when new information is mixed or integrated with old information, it can reshape attitudes. Logically, for an attitude to be favorable overall, the positive ideas must be more numerous or have higher weight and value than unfavorable ideas. For example, if you were purchasing a car, your favorable ideas might be things like sporty, nice color, affordable, and handles well. However, that same car might also have poor gas mileage, little trunk room, and a poor stereo. Your overall attitude would depend on how many of these items the car has and which ones are most important to you (weight).

The more cars you see, the sooner your attitudes form based on familiar information. In other words, information and the attitudes around it transfer to the next car-buying situation. You can quickly determine if what you value is achievable. This is another way people draw the line on adjustments when familiar information is involved.

Is there any familiar information that you might be holding on to when working toward your goals? What are they, and might they be stopping you in some way?

_____

_____

_____

_____

_____

_____

Let the Music Play

Remember my music agent friend Mike from chapter 4? He had the skills and ability to remain at his former company, but unfortunately, the bar kept changing for him, and he was fatigued from this. He knew he could be successful with any task in his work. But without clear, achievable goals, it was like he was running without ever reaching the finish line. In addition, traveling all the time was misaligned with his work/life balance beliefs.

Looking back at the five "Fs," which ones would you say caused him to draw the line on adjustments and leave his job? Do you think it was faith? How about fatigue?

Mike actually had three of the five reasons to put the brakes on making further adjustments to achieve inside the company he was working for and find a new opportunity. They were faith, fatigue, and the familiar. Now you can see why he made the decision he did. He had the talent and the ability to do the job, but he knew that he had to stay true to his faith, family, and himself. Leaving his job created an adjustment in and of itself. But the old saying holds: "When God closes a door, He opens a window." In leaving the job, Mike became his own boss and is able to do what he loves and be there for his family.

One might say that when we draw the line on some adjustments, we open the door to others. Let's look at how adjustments can open doors for you in the next chapter!

CHAPTER 11

Great Adjustments Open Doors

"Look before, or you'll always find yourself behind."

—BENJAMIN FRANKLIN

Swinging for the Fences

Have you ever been in a job interview where you felt like you wished you had something groundbreaking to share, but nothing came to mind? How about a situation where a friend is going through something uncertain and turns to you for your thoughts? Wouldn't it be nice to be able to speak confidently in these situations? From my experience, it's safe to say that once someone knows more about adjustments, they suddenly feel empowered in new ways.

If you're thinking, "That sounds great, but I'm not sure I understand the adjustment topic enough to talk about it," you're not alone. This is a new concept for almost everyone. And it will take a little practice to use it to your advantage—especially since many people equate the word adjustments with chiropractic care and spinal movement! While that is true in the medical world, it is so much more than that.

Let me paint a picture as to how this might look. Imagine you go to work on a Monday and find out that your company plans to roll out a new computer platform over the next few weeks. Everything you do will be changing. This requires an adjustment. For most people, this could cause some anxiety or panic.

Let's pretend that, from the Adjustment Awareness Audit, you found that you have more Steady Eddy tendencies than other pattern types. This means that you might be inclined to talk to others about how they feel about the new change. You may be curious about it, but you may take a skeptical attitude, depending on how other implementations went in the past. Finally, while you don't mind deadlines, you prefer to keep the same pace of work.

By knowing your adjustment tendencies, you know how you would react to this new situation, which may provide some comfort and peace. However, the change is coming, and next week, you have two choices. You can allow your natural pattern to play itself out, or you can optimize your pattern. The first choice would seem to be easier because it doesn't require additional effort and is comfortable. You don't need to focus on the big picture because you can just work through the tasks in front of you. But you may find that choosing this path ends up making you more anxious if there are tight deadlines and little guidance from management.

However, if you decide to optimize your pattern in this situation, what would that look like, and could that open doors? Just for fun, let's say you decided to do only two new things: take a more offensive strategic position and increase knowledge about the platform. If you did just those two small optimizations, you could impact the overall success of the platform rollout. By being offensive, you take your timing and, therefore, your accountability into your own hands. You push yourself when no one else is. By increasing your knowledge of the platform, you can push yourself more because you know what the platform can and cannot do. This gives you information about other offensive strategies. You will also be able to teach others, which aligns with the social aspect of the Steady Eddy.

If the launch is successful, and you were part of its success, even in a small way, you may be asked to assist with other projects or be given priority for promotion or lateral moves. In addition, you might help make the lives of your coworkers a little easier. I would say those are doors opened!

If after that one successful optimization event, you decide never again to optimize your pattern, it will return to its natural state. However, once you experience the power of pattern optimization, you may begin to see how you can gain control and impact your life (and that of others) in new ways. Now, that's a home run and something to talk about!

The Post-Game Interview

The first time I was asked to help an international player prepare for an interview, I was excited. I was given past interviews and time with the team reporter looking over typical questions. I spent months getting the right curriculum together and prepping the player by asking him to answer the questions in his own words first, then translating missing words for him to English. It was important that he spoke from his heart, even though he didn't have all the words or verb tenses down pat. This Cuban player was considered a top prospect but hadn't spent enough time in the language program to have command yet, so this was a special circumstance. In addition, he had a few linguistic challenges, so we had to work a little harder to overcome them. I tried, of course, to help him overcome the language barrier so that he could express himself in English. But more than that, I tried to dispel any fears he might have felt about using his "voice"—not just the one that came out of his throat but the one that shared the way he saw the world.

If you think about it, isn't that a challenge for all of us? We all have various perspectives of the world, but do we share those? Maybe we don't for fear of what others may think. Or maybe we don't think others will care. But sharing the world through our eyes is an important part of connection, culture, and progress.

One of the things I learned in preparing players for interviews was that reporters want to know how the player prepared to succeed in the game and what they were thinking when there was a mishap or error. This is the heart of adjustment, isn't it? Why do reporters want to know this? Because it tells us more about the person and what he was thinking and doing in order for us to learn, be inspired, or satisfy our curiosity. Don't we want to know how people do things and why? Once we find out how a player responds in a game, we connect with him. He opened the door to our interest, and now we may follow him on social media or google him.

The world wants to know how you adjust because everyone is trying to adjust to things every day. They want to know if you know what you're doing. They want to know how you become excellent. They want to know if this may be able to help them at some point. What will you tell them? Will you share that you fumble through things, or will you tell them that you have a plan for change and uncertainty in your life? What if you told them that you have been working on adjustment skills based on your natural tendencies? Wouldn't they be surprised?! Can you imagine what a prospective employer or client would say if they saw how confident you were in handling change, uncertainty, and even failure? That's how great adjustments open doors to more conversation, more opportunities, and more growth.

The Scout

Every interviewer is like a baseball scout, looking for great talent. In fact, we are all scouts in some way. We could be looking for an employee, or we could be looking for a great plumber, a friend, or even a spouse. When we look at what's important to us, we may have a list of things besides skill or performance ability. But no matter what's on that list, it will likely be tested under life's ever-changing conditions.

When my son Nick was interviewing for a job after college, he had many interviews. One in particular stood out to him. It was one year before the COVID-19 pandemic, and he had to visually record himself answering questions that popped up on his laptop. He didn't have much time to think through his answers, and that was what the company wanted. The last question they asked him was really interesting to me. He was asked, "What else do we need to know about you?" This question was different from all the other ones and was meant to see what the interviewee would find important about him/herself. The interviewee had to decide whether to share something that spoke to his experience, skills, or something personal.

Nick decided to share something about his personality, and he used examples in his answer. He indirectly spoke about adjustment as it related to people skills because he knew that if he was too direct, it might not be understood. Which adjustment elements did Nick weave in regarding social skills? Strategy, information synthesis, and beliefs. He was hired.

Whether you're looking to succeed in an interview or help adjust to a new software platform at work, the elements are useful to know, optimize, and talk about.

I think of adjustments as the key to opening a door. Doors give us a way to move from one place to another and see into other areas that we may not have had the chance to see otherwise. Without doors, we are stuck in one place. We may want to be in that place, which may be a comfortable and good place. Or we may not want to be there. We may want to be able to move between both places, even for a time, which is possible with a door.

Maybe you're standing behind a door that you are hoping will open. Are you waiting for someone on the other side of the door to open it? Maybe that will be the case. Perhaps you need to unlock the door first. Unlocking a door is simply talking about adjustment elements and using them in your own life. You can open the door by using those elements to persevere through challenges, stay disciplined, be trustworthy, encourage others, and be hopeful about whatever situation you are working through.

In baseball, players hope that a scout will come and open the door for them. But the truth is, the door is opened through their actions first. Perhaps this is the case for you too.

The Ninth Inning

I recently heard someone say that adults don't really win and certainly don't get trophies. They just do what is needed and keep grinding through life. I guess that depends on your idea of winning.

A good friend of mine in baseball once told me that games are not won in the first part of the game; they are won in the seventh, eighth, and ninth innings. The reason is that energy levels are lower, anxiety grows, and players have less time to make smart adjustments. Winning becomes a matter of staying disciplined (in the mind as well as the body) and adjusting well through the entire game. While it can be a grind to do this, winning is more achievable.

This is the same in life. If we stay focused on great adjustments until our goals are complete, we improve our odds of winning. Winning isn't all about trophies. It's about facing life's challenges with confidence, security, and joy while growing as a person. How are you facing life right now? Do you feel confident about how you move through change? Do you feel secure in your abilities and who you are? How much joy are you feeling? Could this be improved? If you were great in all of these areas, would you feel like you were winning? I bet you would.

Whether you have the tendencies of an All-Star, a Maverick, a Free Agent, or any other of the other adjustment patterns, you can win at your life. You may need to learn how to grow your elements and utilize them better, but everybody usually does. Winning is possible for all of us, and no door is too heavy or thick when we are well-equipped.

In the title of this book, I've used "million dollar" to signify successful adjustments and those that make successful adjustments. But in reality, money is not the only measure of a successful adjustment or a successful life.

Benjamin Franklin once said, "Look before or you'll always find yourself behind." When you know more about how you make adjustments in times of change, uncertainty, or failure, you are opening a door to the future and not worrying about what you might find there. You can clearly see the room that you've been in for a while and which doors you've been keeping closed. This information has the power to transform you because you realize, perhaps for the first time, that you now have a key to the doors you choose to unlock. Opening doors and moving through new spaces builds confidence and grows you as a person, perhaps allowing you to help others do the same.

Through this growth you can master your talent and increase your endurance. Fear is less powerful because you aren't focused on one outcome anymore. You realize that you just simply have to tweak one of your five elements in order to create your win. Is this difficult or unrealistic? No. In fact, quite the opposite. It is:

Doable.

Sustainable.

Practical.

Scalable.

Empowering.

Want to increase performance in any area? Be more productive and satisfied? Have more peace? Whether you're in the minor league or the major league of your life, early in the game or late in the game, you have the key now. It's one pitch, one bat at a time and one day at a time. Remember that success isn't just one single achievement. It's continual, it's ongoing. It's not just one inning. It's over the entire game, the entire series, and the entire season.

What are you waiting for? The ninth inning is here. Go out, make million dollar adjustments, and win this game!

Acknowledgments

Putting words out into the world is humbling. It is both a responsibility and an honor. Writing this book caused me to spend much time in prayer. All of the experiences that I had that led up to this book, as well as the people I met and the knowledge that I was given was only because of God, and I did nothing special to earn it. This book is dedicated to Him and His Son, Jesus Christ.

There were many who made this book possible, and I need to offer my deepest thanks. I want to start with my incredible family for their unending love and support in this process.

Jon, thank you for your encouragement, patience, and interest in my work with education, baseball, adjustment testing, and, of course, writing this book. Thank you for suggesting we travel to that first spring training so many years ago and offering such great business counsel behind the scenes throughout the years. I could not have done any of this without your support. You are an incredible husband, father, friend, and mentor, and I love you so much.

Jordan, thank you for being the first author in the family— I learned so much from you! Thank you for putting me in touch with Peter Licalzi who helped me get started and for all the encouragement and fun conversations about writing. It has been invigorating to be able to share this with you! Also, thank you for allowing me to tell a small part of your story here as well. I love you for that, but also for who you are. I pray God's blessings on you always.

Matt, thank you for being a beacon of support to Jordan and this family. You had to listen to countless conversations and take my test over and over again, and I appreciate your patience and support! I love you for all you do and who you are—it is seen, noticed, and so appreciated. May God bless you always as well.

Nick, where would the Signature PAR test be without you? Your strategic mind was such a huge help in the beginning as test setups were tested. Your constant willingness to help and easygoing personality are such incredible blessings to me and so many others. Thank you for all you did behind the scenes in big and small ways. I love you for the amazing person you are, and I ask God's blessings on you always.

Allie—while you're the newest person in the family, I have already grown to love you. Thank you for being so caring and kind. May God always bless you!

To Hatuey Mendoza—where do I begin? You are not just an incredible human being, you are a brother to me and your family is my family. Your work ethic and heart for players gave me the desire to give 200 percent. Thank you for giving me the opportunity to serve them well.

To Greg Long and Jill Long de Mercado—nothing happens on accident. Meeting you and knowing you both has been part of a bigger plan to have an international impact on the world, and I am blessed by you both. Greg, thank you for allowing me to step into that first press box and Jill, thank you for being so passionate about player education and making the work so much more fun! You are like a sister to me.

To all the incredible men who I work with in the baseball world, thank you for being such positive role models for young men today. You don't get much thanks for all you do, but I see it and I know the players see it too. You grind it out every day to make them better and that kind of work is divinely blessed.

Thank you to Dr. John Lubker, Nick Scope, and McKinsey Cummings for being part of the initial testing team. Your passion and interest in the cognitive data sciences and your willingness to go the extra mile to prove theories and validate findings was invaluable.

Thank you to my extended family, friends, and neighbors who encouraged me and lifted me up throughout this entire process. I am lucky to have you all in my life and I appreciate every one of you.

Finally, I want to thank my agent, Shannon Marven, and all the hard-working people at Dupree Miller. Your belief in this project was very much appreciated, and I am blessed to work with all of you.

About the Author

Author Photo by Scott Leonard

Linda Wawrzyniak is a learning and human development expert who has worked with high performance organizations, such as the Chicago Cubs and other professional baseball organizations. She was involved in the 2016 World Series player development department, helping them improve team communication and connection. She is an expert in transitioning multicultural talent from around the globe, which requires thousands of adjustments. Former students include players such as Willson Contreras, Eloy Jiménez, and Ender Inciarte, a 2016 Golden Glove winner.

Linda is the founder of Higher Standards Academy, LLC, and Major League Consulting, LLC. In a unique position to be one of the first to create learning products for international professional baseball players, she created the V+1 Transition System and the PAR test of adjustment, to name a few. These tools have helped organizations not only identify top talent in the MLB draft, but also provide tools to help professional athletes and many others outside of sports perform more quickly at their highest level possible.